REBUILT to DOMINATE

Le'Charles Bentley

ISBN 13: 978-1986410861

ISBN-10: 1986410862

DEDICATION

This book is dedicated to my children, Le'Charles, Antonio, Vernon, Charles, Rozalia, and Andre. Each of you represents in your own special ways the best parts of myself. I challenge each of you to always love and support one another. The world you are growing up in is rapidly changing. Your biggest hurdles will be staying true to who you are and to never forget the power all of you hold inside you. Trust your instincts, fight for what you believe in, be proud of who you are, and never let anything come in between you.

CONTENTS

1 CHAPTER

BROKEN

The fateful words from the head team orthopedic surgeon were: "LeCharles, this is a life-and-limb-threatening situation. We are going to prepare for surgery. The nurse will bring you down in 10 minutes."

The team of surgeons then all turned and walked out of the door. I immediately felt no pain. Those sobering words brought me to a reality I was not ready to face at 26 years of age. He told me there was a chance I was going to die or lose my leg.

But that's not what I heard.

I heard this, "You will never be able to play football again."

Here I was, staring my human mortality in the face, but the only thing I could process was the idea of not being able to play football as an amputee. So, I had 10 minutes to figure some things out.

I asked everyone to leave the room. I needed to be alone.

Here I am, 26, one of the best in the world at my job, living out my childhood dream, and now being told I was potentially going to die. This was a curveball. I guess my self-diagnosed flu is a bit more than I thought. But what is it? I still had no idea as to why my "life and limb" was being threatened.

It didn't matter. I had ten minutes to reconcile with the fact I was staring death in the face. I wanted to cry. But it was a waste of valuable time at that moment. I wanted more answers. But the answers would change nothing at that moment. I wanted to be angry. But anger wasn't going to fix anything at that moment. Nothing was going to change the fact I was headed into a surgery where the doctors were not confident I would live through it, and if I had lived through it, they surely were going to remove my leg.

Fuck that. I needed a plan. In my mind, I had options.

Option A was death.

Option B was amputee.

I know, you're thinking, "LeCharles, no, this is your reality, you don't get to choose your reality."

Well, you are wrong, because I made a choice. I decided I would rather die than lose my leg. If I lost my leg, my football career was over. Nobody wants to sign a football player with one leg. If my football career is over, then what's left for me?

I wasn't ready to be some sad story on ESPN about the "hometown boy who tragically lost his leg." A few sad articles and text messages from former teammates telling me how much they feel "sorry" for me. Then everyone forgets about me while I spend the rest of my life trying to adapt to life as an amputee.

I didn't sign up for this shit. So I decided death was the more noble option.

But how in the hell was I going to pull this off? I had five minutes. I've never had a suicidal thought a day in my life. But at this moment, I was ready to die.

I devised a plan that was so selfish it still embarrasses me to this day. There was zero thought about the anguish my mother was feeling. I was her baby boy. My family stood in the hallway dealing with inconceivable fright. It didn't faze me.

I was a father. There wasn't any concern about my two sons seeing their daddy in a casket. They have a great mother and money. They can visit me at the graveyard. It's all good.

Something I wanted so badly was about to potentially be taken away from me. If I couldn't play football, I would rather be dead.

These words aren't written with the underscore of chest thumping male bravado.

I was selfish. I was a quitter. I was a coward. Underneath all of the success and physical strength was an insecure and self-centered harebrained fool. My inner drive took me down an extremely dark road. I had no idea how consumed I had become with chasing my goals. The compass seemed to be pointing in a positive direction; instead it was guiding me straight to hell.

My entire life changed on what should have been one of the most exciting days of my life: the first day of training camp playing for my hometown team, the Cleveland Browns. I had signed with the Browns as a free agent in the offseason, and vowed to bring greatness to the team I grew up watching. That day in August, 2006, was a typical hot and humid Cleveland summer day. I marched to the line of scrimmage on the first play of inside run drill. The play was outside zone.

It started as any other play. I surveyed the defensive front seven, identified the Mike linebacker, and crouched down to get in position to make my line call to direct the front side and backside guards on what I felt was the most effective way to block the three-four defensive front our team ran.

I clearly understood what my role was going to be in Cleveland. I was signed to make the jobs of the other players around me easier. All the teams in the division ran 3-4 defenses, and all were anchored by big men like Casey Hampton in Pittsburgh. My responsibility was to make the defenses in the division play with ten men on the field each week. It's rare to have a center who can consistently single block nose guards, and I was one of the centers who could. This would free the guards to take on the linebackers who were at a physical disadvantage when matched up with guards in the run game.

The line call that was written into the blocking scheme was an "A" block. This is where I would work with the backside guard to double team the nose guard; as I did that, I worked up to the backside linebacker. The blocking scheme works just fine, but it's not nearly as effective as a "man" approach. This is where the center takes the nose guard on a single block, and both guards immediately attack the linebackers.

I reached down to grab the football, did my usual roll of the ball to get the front of laces perfectly positioned at the tip of my middle finger.

I called "man." The backside guard, Joe Andruzzi, said "we should 'A' it!" I wasn't having any of that. The call was "man." I felt the quarterback position his hands under my crotch, my breathing slowed down, and the only thing I could hear was the quarterback barking through the cadence. My mind and body knew it was go time.

Many players were coached to target physical "landmarks" on the defender to give themselves a spot to attack that would give them the best chance to win the matchup, but I never liked looking at the defenders. Defenders moved. When they moved, so did your target. I wanted to target something that I could lock my sight on before taking my shot.

There was a small brown patch of grass that I locked my eyes on that was just outside the left heel of Ted Washington, who to this day is the largest human being I have ever seen. Ted and I had battled one another the season prior when he was with the Raiders, and I was with the Saints. I was very familiar with his game.

The quarterback was coming to the end of his cadence. I could feel my hamstrings get tight. I was ready to explode toward that small patch of brown grass. "Set HIT." My right arm violently jerked back to deliver the ball to the quarterback's waiting hands. The snap was clean. My eyes were locked onto that brown patch of grass, but I could feel where everyone around me was exactly located. The field was a big chessboard in my mind. I didn't have to see everything to see everything.

My right foot hit the ground with violence. My left foot hit the ground, then I suddenly felt like someone had kicked me. I felt myself begin to fall. In my mind, I'm cussing my backside guard because I thought he ignored my "man" call, executed an "A" block, and somehow got himself tangled with my left leg. Boy, I was going to read him the riot act once we got back to the huddle.

My helmet drove directly into the dirt. Boom, I was on the ground. My anger at Joe Andruzzi didn't allow me to recognize what had truly happened. My patellar tendon had ripped apart.

The anger quickly dissipated and turned to anguish as I felt a burning sensation in my left leg like I had never felt before. I grabbed my knee, but could no longer feel my kneecap. I knew something was terribly wrong. It was almost instinctual to roll over to the fetal position while I clenched my left knee.

The burn slowly intensified. I could feel a hand on my lower back. It was the team trainer. He was telling me to breathe and relax. They needed me to roll over to my back so they could determine what exactly was wrong. Two prevailing lines of thought consumed me. First, the pain was too great to move, and I felt safe curled up with both of my hands tightly clinched around my left knee. Second, I was afraid to know what was wrong. There was comfort in the mystery. Was there blood? Did a bone break through my skin? I didn't want to see that.

I could feel tears welling up in my eyes. Oh no, my teammates are going to see me crying. This is all bad. Maybe I should have called the "A" block. Once the team medical staff was able to pry me out of the fetal position I was sitting on the ground, and I just so happened to catch a glance of my kneecap.

It was resting midway up my thigh.

I knew this wasn't good..

2 CHAPTER

THE BEST TWEET THAT NEVER HAPPENED

Twitter really hadn't taken wing in 2006. It was around, but had not erupted into the world's first real-time news feed that it is today. If it were as popular then as it is now, the Cleveland Browns would have tweeted from its official blue checked account: "LeCharles Bentley has undergone a successful knee operation."

Assuredly there would have been hundreds of replies with well wishes and emoji's of praying hands. The tweet would not have qualified as fake news. The surgery was successful. My patellar tendon had been successfully repaired.

This wasn't my first knee operation. I had suffered an ACL tear in the same knee in 2003 while playing with the Saints. This previous surgery created a slightly unique set of circumstances for my future patellar repair. In 2003, my ACL repair was completed with a patellar tendon autograft. This is a fancy way of saying that a small sliver of my patellar tendon was harvested to use it as a replacement ACL.

Imagine taking a sheet of paper, cutting out a thin piece in the middle of the paper, and then gluing the paper back together; this about sums up a patellar tendon autograft. It's a common surgery for orthopedics when dealing with active patients, because it creates a stronger ACL repair. That said, it can increase chances for a subsequent patellar tendon rupture.

It's completely logical. You compromise the integrity of one area to make another area stronger; the compromised area is now at a higher risk to be further compromised. This is the reality of being an athlete. It's also why high quality rehab is paramount to an athlete's return to play.

My rehabilitation following my 2003 ACL repair left a bit to be desired. All of my rehab was done under the New Orleans Saints training staff at the time. Looking back, this was not the best thing for me, which is why I strongly advise players against rehabbing with their teams. There aren't any unconscionable details to reveal about the Saints training staff. They did the best they could under the system in which they work.

The business of the NFL, by its nature, is not compelled to provide the highest quality therapy practices available. Does this mean that teams don't care about their players' well being? No, because some do. It simply means the business model of the NFL doesn't create a need for teams to think long term about a player's health. The model is designed to keep a player functional.

When team doctors, trainers, and therapists are constantly under pressure to get players "healthy" as quickly as possible, there tends to be an elevated sense of urgency and a willingness to cut corners. We then place young, naive, and shortsighted men with non-guaranteed contracts in an environment where their availability to perform is often the greatest barrier between being a Pro Bowler or out of the NFL. It creates a potentially toxic environment for medical practices.

My ACL rehab was a bit rushed. Am I blaming the Saints or the NFL? Hell no. I wanted to get back healthy more than anyone in the world. Most players after ACL surgery are physically, mentally, and emotionally out of commission for quite some time. I was in the weight room at 6 a.m. the next morning with 225 pounds on the bar doing a bench press with my leg propped up on a box. In my mind at the time, it was a great way to sweat out the anesthesia and stay strong.

Looking back, I was a raging lunatic. But my lunacy was partly why, in my second year in the NFL, I had already been voted Sports Illustrated Rookie of the Year and Pro Bowl alternate as a rookie. Why I was coming off my first Pro Bowl berth as a guard, and was preparing to move to center for my third year. I had to get the knee right. I refused to let it slow me down. Getting "healthy" wasn't the solution. I had to get back to being "functional," and that's what I did.

I pushed to get back on the field quickly and it hurt me. It's highly common to develop tendonitis after a patellar tendon autograft. Let's think … a slice of the tendon was removed. This places more pressure on the overall integrity of the tendon. When you're a 310-pound professional athlete who earns a living by crashing your body into bodies of other 300-plus-pound men, there's an increased chance of inflammation.

Ultimately, that's what tendonitis is. The suffix 'itis' in medical jargon means inflammation; therefore tendonitis literally means inflammation of a tendon. That's what I had developed. In the grand scheme of all that can medically go wrong with players in the NFL, tendonitis is akin to krill in an ocean full of great white sharks, and it's treated that way. It's something players work around. Remember, the NFL is about "functional," not "healthy." But when tendonitis graduates from acute to chronic, that's a sign to take your foot off the gas and address the problem, not just the symptoms. Well, my tendonitis had graduated cum laude. At this point it was time to devise a management plan, but a key element to managing tendonitis is rest. The word "rest" in the NFL is like "snow" in hell. It doesn't exist.

I hadn't missed any games or practices with knee issues after the ACL repair. I was "functional." That following season post ACL operation, after moving from guard to center, I was voted as a first alternate to the Pro Bowl in my first season playing center in the NFL. I narrowly missed being voted in, but it's not easy to supplant guys who had been around like Matt Birk and Olin Kreutz. They were the big dogs. I had a secret man crush on Olin Kreutz. This isn't a "coming out of the closet" moment. Olin was simply a player I greatly respected. But I wanted to be better than him and any other center who ever played, so I pushed. I pushed my way onto the 2006 NFL Pro Bowl roster with Kreutz the following season.

At that point I'm not just "functional." I'm elite. My tendonitis was something I was told would just be something I would have to "manage" the rest of my career. OK. As a young athlete aspiring to be "best center of all-time" and walk across the stage in Canton to deliver the Pro Football Hall of Fame speech I had been practicing in my mind for the last five years, the krill of the NFL's oceanic medical food chain was not about to stop me.

Except the tendonitis was no longer krill. It had become a shark that leaped out of my knee and onto the surgical table during my patellar tendon repair in Cleveland. Of course this is hyperbole, but could you imagine the faces of the medical staff if that had truly happened? What would the Browns post-operative tweet look like then?

They'd need way more than 280 characters to explain that shit.

I digress.

Following the initial patellar tendon repair, the Browns team doctor told me that the quality of my patellar tendon was very poor. No, this was not solely because of the prior autograft, but because I had developed tendonosis. Tendonosis is the meaner and stronger big brother of tendonitis, what happens over a period of time when tendonitis in its acute form goes unresolved. Tendonitis morphs into the chronic and much more severe medical condition, tendonosis.

Tendonosis is a more dire condition because chronic inflammation slowly destroys the affected area by impeding collagen production. What is tissue made of? Ding, ding, ding! You got it, collagen. With collagen production hindered, the tissue becomes stringy, and that doesn't bode well for long-term tendon health. The revelation of tendonosis is often made after you are lying on a table with a ruptured tendon, unless you are under the medical guidance of people who aren't merely concerned with "function" and are more interested in addressing long-term health.

This is similar to heart disease. Generally, it's after a medical scare that a heart problem is discovered. Unless, you have a family doctor who is insistent on annual blood work and diligent on checking all of the biomarkers that can reveal a looming heart attack, even when you appear perfectly "healthy." Well, I was a coming off a Pro Bowl season. I passed my exit physical with the Saints. I passed my team physical with the Browns prior to signing the largest contract for a center in the history of the NFL at the time. Yes, this horse was clearly "functional," and that's the baseline prerequisite for staying in the NFL.

The patellar tendon surgery wasn't as simple as stitching back the damaged tendon and sewing my knee back together. There wasn't enough quality tendon left. Envision taking two sheets of paper and running each sheet half way through a paper shredder, then trying to glue the frayed ends of each sheet together. In order to give the surgery the best chance of success, a hamstring tendon was harvested and used to supplement the strength of the total repair.

This addition of the hamstring tendon to a patellar tendon repair is not uncommon. But the preexisting elements made this surgical maneuver imperative. Even under these unique sets of circumstances, "LeCharles Bentley has undergone a successful knee operation." Twelve years later, it's still not fake news. My patellar tendon was repaired, but I was about to be broken.

3 CHAPTER

HOME IS WHERE THE HEART IS

I was afraid to look at my postoperative scar. It scared me. As an athlete you embrace the inherent dangers of what you do. You sign up to get injured. But this felt different. I was embarrassed. I felt as if I had let so many people down.

Growing up in Cleveland, there was a different connection between myself and what the Cleveland Browns represented to so many people. I understood that relationship. I knew what the people in Cleveland wanted. I spent every offseason when I played for the Saints in Cleveland. I owned a home in Cleveland. I sat on the front steps of my Cleveland childhood home and traded phone calls with my agent as the terms of my first NFL contract were being hashed out. This wasn't a casual love affair. It began in childhood, sitting in the barbershop listening to the "old heads" reminisce over the glory days.

There were times I could literally feel the frustrations

with the Browns in the city. But people still loved them. Clevelanders are a prideful and loyal bunch. We are often on the butt end of jokes, but your laughing doesn't faze a real Clevelander, because in our minds we've already kicked your ass, twice.

But now I was in a fight with myself. There was so much fanfare and excitement surrounding my signing in Cleveland. This is where I wanted to be, which is in stark contrast to the desires of many 26-year-old professional athletes. Cleveland? It sucks there. The city is awful. You will never win any games. Those uniforms are hideous. The ole "mistake by the lake."

I heard it all. But I held on to what the city meant to me. Between my junior and senior year of high school, my dad and I drove down to the construction site as the current stadium was being built. My father was interested in the process. I was more interested in the future. As my father pointed out certain construction elements that stood out to him, I told my father, "You watch, I'm going to make you proud and play here one day."

My father had hearing loss, so he either ignored me, or didn't hear me. Either way, I said it, and meant it.

But 10 years later, there I was with a nine inch stitch-laden incision down my left knee sitting in the training room wondering if that promise would go unfulfilled, if my dream of running out of the tunnel as a Cleveland

Brown would ever happen. I wanted to help change the city of Cleveland, but I couldn't even bring myself to look at this hideous scar, because it scared the hell out of me.

But I got my shit together. It didn't take long for me to begin attacking rehab in the same manner I did everything else that got me to that point in my life. At one time during my rehab, I was approximately three months ahead of the scheduled pace. There was chatter about me potentially being able to make it back to play the last few games of the season. The chatter was all from me, but nonetheless, there was chatter.

I'd ask the head trainer to point out the muscles in my quad, so I could write the names down and begin learning more about the function, and importance, of each one. My rehab time quickly turned into class. Anyone who has gone through an extended period of postoperative rehabilitation understands the fact you better quickly figure out ways to keep yourself mentally engaged in the process. If you don't, your mind will sink in to an abyss and your healing will be slowed.

My method of choice was to spend time learning more about my body. I would soon learn something about my body that wasn't on the rehabilitation syllabus.

4 CHAPTER

THEN IT HAPPENED

Four weeks into my rehab, sleeping with my brace off became an option. The team doctors felt I was far enough removed from the procedure to give my leg a breather at night. This was a big milestone. I don't even like sleeping in pajamas, so for me trying to get a good night's rest while wearing a bulky knee brace was nearly impossible.

One morning I woke up, slid myself to the edge of the bed and stood up on my right leg. My brace was lying on the opposite edge of the bed from where I was standing. At that time, it looked like I had to cross the Grand Canyon to reach this thing. I'm not even talking about a California king sized bed. This was a normal king size bed. But when you're four weeks out of patellar tendon surgery, all movement becomes like climbing Mount Everest.

I sat back on the bed and began to laterally scoot myself towards the brace. "Inch by inch life's a cinch…" I called bullshit on that quote this particular morning. It felt like I had run a marathon. Nevertheless, I made it. As I stood up to strap the brace around my left leg, the bulk of my weight was still shifted to my right leg.

This particular brace was the length of my leg. It started at my upper thigh and ended just below my calf. I began to tighten each strap starting from the bottom. As I neared the top towards the last few straps, I began to shift some of the weight on my right leg to my left leg.

Then it happened. My left leg ever so slightly gave out. It wasn't a tumbling down to the ground type of knee buckle. It was a very slight bend of the knee before I caught myself and finished strapping up the brace. In my mind, it wasn't a big deal by any stretch of the imagination. I had regained a significant amount of knee flexion, and that slight jerk was nowhere close to the ranges of motion that had been established in rehab.

Once I arrived at the facility for therapy, I let the team trainer know what had happened. It wasn't because I was concerned, more because I felt good about being able to catch myself before anything truly catastrophic happened. The trainer wasn't overly impressed. An intern drove me down to the Cleveland Clinic to get some ultrasound imaging done on the area. This seemed to be overkill, but there was a lot at stake. I understood.

To everyone's surprise, there was now a five-millimeter tear in the tendon repair. My father was a carpenter, but I only knew there were 12 inches in a foot and ten yards for a first down. I needed clarity on what a five-millimeter tear looked like. The team doctor shrugged his shoulders and said, "It's tiny. It will heal as the graft heals." It was far from a big deal at the time. Ironically, a tiny five-millimeter tear was about to reveal a much more grave reality.

Because the next morning I felt sick. The weather in Cleveland was beginning to shift away from the hot and muggy summer days toward chillier fall-like temperatures. Maybe it was the weather change that had me feeling a little unlike myself. My knee was also sore. I rolled over to call the head trainer to let him know I wasn't feeling too well, and ask if I should take the day off considering we were so far ahead of schedule.

"LCB, my man, what's going on?" he asked.

"Hey, I don't feel too well. You think I could get the day off?" I said.

The phone got quiet. It was one of those, "Hey, my period is late" kind of quiets. It was the kind of quiet that makes both parties uncomfortable. At the time, I didn't think much of it.

"You know, you should come in and let us check you out," he said.

In my head, my response was, "hell no." But the words

that came out of my mouth were, "OK, can I come in a little later? I'm going to drink some cough medicine and lay back down to see if I can shake it off."

It was all good. We agreed I could show up in a few hours. My mother brought me some cough syrup and eggs, a breakfast for champions. I watched a little television, then dozed back to sleep.

I awoke again about two hours later. It was still mid-morning. My knee had swollen to about the size of a softball and I felt like a train had hit me.

I reached for the phone to call the team trainer.

"Hey, I feel awful. I can't make it today," I said.

This time there wasn't any uncomfortable pause.

"You need to come in, immediately," he said.

My knee felt like it had a heartbeat of its own. The flu? This was the worst case of the flu I ever had.

"Nah, I am going back to sleep," I said.

"LCB, you need to get here right now," he said, sternly.

Generally, I don't take too kindly to people demanding I do something, but this wasn't him being an asshole. I heard the concern in his voice.

The trip from the bedroom to the car was one of the most

painful things I have ever endured. In my mind, this was a mere case of the flu and me pushing too hard in rehab. I just needed to rest.

I was nearly dead wrong. My mother got me to the Browns headquarters, about a 20-minute ride. By the time we made it to the facility, my self-diagnosed flu had gotten exponentially worse. I refused to leave the car. The pain was too much.

The head trainer came out to the car. I wasn't feeling well, but my instincts were operating just fine. The look on his face told me there was something they were concerned about. He wanted me to head over to a branch of the Cleveland Clinic in Strongsville, Ohio, for a blood test.

"Are you fucking kidding me? A blood test? Bro, it's the flu, calm down," I said.

My mother took over.

"No, I'm taking him there right now," she said.

"Great, I will call you later this afternoon to check in," he said.

I said, "Fuck both of you." It was in my head, so nobody heard it, but I did say it with authority. The words just never actually came out of my mouth, because if my mother did hear those words directed at her, I would have had a black eye to go along with my self-diagnosed flu.

Later that day I was back home when my phone rang.

"You need to get to the Cleveland Clinic, right now," the head trainer said.

I had gone to get my blood work as instructed, and was back in bed. The phone rang approximately three hours after we had arrived back home. My mother just happened to be in the room when I answered. Had she not been in the room, I would have hung up the phone, and rolled over to go back to sleep.

She took the phone from me.

"Ok, we are headed there now," she said.

But we had a problem, I couldn't walk. Boy, this flu was kicking my ass. By the grace of God, my brother-in-law, sister, and my brother were at the house. They carried me to the car. My knee had swollen to the size of a basketball.

My body's internal thermostat was somehow set on "hell hot." But at the same time I was shivering cold. I didn't know there were leprechauns in Cleveland who rode deer. Well, apparently there are. I saw them. Or at least in my mind I did. I was hallucinating.

My knee seemed to take on a life of its own. I could feel it pulsating and swelling in real time. Each bump in the road felt like a bomb exploded inside my knee joint. By the time we arrived at the hospital, the pain got to the point where it literally felt like a jackhammer was pounding away at my entire body. I kept thinking to myself, "This flu is kicking my ass." I had zero clue about the level of danger I was truly in. Until I heard those words from the team doctor that would forever change my life.

My brother-in-law wheeled me up to a room inside the Cleveland Clinic. It was a little larger than a typical patient room, but nothing fancy. As I sat in the wheelchair, a nurse began poking me with a needle to start an IV. She couldn't find a vein. I played along as her human pincushion for as long as I could.

"Um, I'm good. Just bring me some water," I said.

She was visibly frustrated. The entire room felt morbid. The faces of my family as they sat in the room with me were all faces of concern. My mother was eerily quiet. I couldn't figure out why there was so much concern over the flu. Grab me a bottle of NyQuil and slide me two Percocet. I will sleep this thing off.

That is what I genuinely believed, until I looked up and saw a train of doctors walking through the door, led by the team's head orthopedic surgeon. He was the only familiar face. The other doctors, I had no clue who they were. But I counted a total of 10. You read that correctly.

There were 10 doctors in the room.

At this moment, I knew some shit was wrong. They all lined up along the wall as if they were taking a prom group photo. I vividly remember the faces. They all looked as if someone had died. Little did I know they thought someone was about to die.

That someone was me.

And that's when I decided my life wasn't worth living.

5 CHAPTER

READY TO DIE

The plan was set. I was going to die. It was a Spartan-like plan, but cut me some slack. I only had 10 minutes to process a bitter reality. My chosen method of execution was anesthesia overdose.

You're probably thinking, "How in the hell were you planning to pull that off?" I didn't have access to anesthesia in the room, but in a very short period of time I was going to be put under for surgery. Well, what if I refused to follow the instructions of the medical staff to "relax" once the gas mask was placed over my nose and mouth? Potentially I could inhale too much. Then, call the pallbearer.

Did I have any medical background or insight to base the prudence of this plan upon? Hell no. I knew two things. One, patients dying from anesthesia overdose was rare. Two, it happens.

I had been through two previous surgical procedures, so I was somewhat familiar with the routine. A gas mask would be placed over my face. I'd be instructed to count backwards from 10 and then I'd wake up in a recovery room.

Surgery is almost like magic. You don't remember anything and you don't feel anything, hopefully. But how much gas was too much? I didn't know. Was I sure this would work? I had no clue. What I was surely confident in was the fact I was damn sure going to try. Hey, you won't make 100 percent of the shots you don't take, right? This was my Hail Mary pass to end the game of life.

The nurse walked through the door. It was go time. Looking back on it, the thing that was so strange to me was the fact I did not pray. I grew up in a deeply religious family, attended Catholic schools from junior high school through high school. Some of my fondest childhood memories were from times spent in church.

I thought I had a great relationship with Christ. But I realized in the most trying time of my life how feeble my faith truly was. It's easy to have faith when you're on top of the world. The challenge is to exercise said faith when life presents us hardship. Faith isn't faith when it's contingent upon things going the way you want them to. *True faith is an unrelenting belief regardless of how dire your circumstances may be.* "Thy will" is being done, and it's our job to trust in the process.

At this moment, I placed trust in my plan, not the Lord's. The nurse began to wheel me toward the elevators. My family tried to hug me and wish me well, but I hadn't acknowledged a single person. My mind was made up. The elite level focus that took me to performance heights many athletes dream of had taken over my spirit. I was a horse with blinders on headed down the track. I was numb.

The elevator ride seemed to take forever. I was anxious. My only fear was my plan failing. The elevator arrived at the basement. When the doors opened, there was an immediate temperature change. It felt like an icebox.

There was an immediate left turn off the elevator, a quick right turn, and then a sharp left turn leading me down a long and dimly lit hallway.

It felt like I was in a scene from a horror movie. There was a long row of hanging white bowl lights that were ever so slightly swaying. The slight swing of the lights created moving shadows along the walls of the hallway. This shit was creepy.

As the nurse wheeled me toward the end of the hallway, I could see there were three surgeons lined up against the wall on the right side of me, and the door to the operating room was on the left. One of the three surgeons was the head team orthopedic surgeon. The other two I didn't recognize.

Neither of them looked at me. It didn't matter to me. I was hoping this was the last time I would ever see them again. The nurse steered me in to the operation room. It was even colder than the rest of the basement.

To my surprise, the head team trainer was standing near the surgery table dressed in medical scrubs. He was there for support. I actually appreciated that. This was no time for me to be angry with anyone. That would all come later.

The beeping of the machines inside the room was loud. There was a rhythm, beep, beep, boop – beep, beep, boop – beep,

beep, boop. This would become the rhythm I would pattern my breathing around once the gas mask was placed over my face.

It took three people to help me from the wheelchair to the operating table.

"You're going to be just fine," the head team trainer whispered to me.

He had no idea what was in my head. I was initially positioned on the table in a sitting position. My torso was upright. This was going better than I thought, because I knew by being in this position I had a better chance of fighting the gas, thus potentially inhaling too much. If I were on my back, I would be more relaxed and that's where the anesthesia can creep up on you.

This anesthesia and me were about to go toe to toe. The gas mask was placed over my face, beep – *deep breath* – beep – *deep breath* – boop – *deep breath*, repeat. I was about five cycles into my breathing pattern when I heard one of the female nurses say, "He needs to relax."

This is working out just fine. A few more breathing cycles. Another voice. "We need to get him to lay down and relax."

This was the voice of a man I didn't recognize. I could feel the concern in the room increasing.

"LCB, you have to relax," the head trainer said.

I was well on my way.

Where was I headed? I had no clue and it didn't matter.

The concern in the room grew stronger. The beeping got louder. My breathing got deeper. The head trainer positioned himself to my left side.

"Relax, you're fine," he said in a very soft voice.

His right hand was on my left shoulder. The concern in the room leaped another level. It was getting intense. Suddenly, I felt someone pull me backwards by my shoulders towards the table. This broke my breathing cycle. I was out.

6 CHAPTER

YOU'RE NOT OUT OF THE WOODS YET

My eyes opened.

An older white lady wearing a white nurse's cap was standing over me. There were all white curtains surrounding my bed. I had to be in heaven.

Groggily I mumbled to the nurse, "Am I alive?"

She said matter of factly, "Of course you are."

This wasn't good. If I were alive, my plan had failed, therefore…. I was an amputee.

I then asked her, "Do I have both of my legs?"

She lifted the bottom of my blanket.

"There's number one, and there's number two. Yup, you are whole," she said.

Ok, I'm alive, I have two legs, great, I will be back playing football in no time. The nurse poured me some water. I dozed off to sleep.

When I awoke again I was in my permanent room, surrounded by the same people I was so prepared to never see again, my family.

This wasn't a "normal" room. This particular floor of the hospital was generally reserved for highbrow patients. Often, royalty from the Middle East would make the trek to Cleveland for surgeries at the Cleveland Clinic, and this floor was reserved for that echelon of patients.

It wasn't the Ritz Carlton, but it was a significant step up from typical hospital rooms. The most significant aspect of the room was the size. It was large enough to comfortably hold six or seven of my family members. This would be key for a couple of reasons. First, I would never be short on visiting family members. Second, this room would be my home for approximately the next eight weeks. Yea, I was in bad shape.

I had a MRSA infection and was suffering from septicemia. MRSA (methicillin resistant staphylococcus aureus) is a strand of staph bacteria that is fully capable of killing you, especially when it reaches the level of septicemia, which is effectively blood poisoning.

The mortality rate for MRSA at the septicemia levels is usually around 20 to 50 percent. I was knocking on death's door.

Instead of removing my leg, the doctors attempted to

save my limb by performing a debridement. This is when infected tissue is surgically removed to give the patient an opportunity to heal. Infections will prevent healing. I'd discover more about this later.

The initial debridement was performed, but the wound was left open, because a second debridement procedure was planned. The wound was packed full of gauze and an infection pump was attached. This pump was designed to suck out as much of the infection as it could. I didn't feel the pump working, but I could see the remnants of its work in a clear plastic bag that was attached to my bed.

It was disgusting. My leg was sliced open, there was a vacuum sucking a killer infection out of my knee, and this was the least of my medical concerns.

The concern for me at this time was the infection potentially attacking key organs like my heart, liver, brain, lungs, or any other area that would create a much more significant problem than an infected knee joint.

Remember, I was dealing with septicemia; this was much bigger than a knee infection. My blood was poisoned; my entire body was fair game at that point. The head team orthopedic surgeon reminded me of the severity of my situation during his daily visits by saying, "You're not out of the woods, yet."

I heard those eerie words for weeks. The doctors did not

know if I was going to live through this. I'd lie in the bed, watching television, clicking my morphine drip when the pain got unbearable. I'd watch nurses switch out bags of antibiotics and wonder if I was going to make it. I went from concocting a plan to kill myself to being deathly afraid I wasn't going to live. The emotional pendulum had swung in a new direction. I wanted to live.

This may all seem warm and fuzzy, that I had come to my senses, that I realized how much my family cared for me, and life was so much bigger than football. Well, sorry, the warm and fuzzy stuff comes later.

I was still a selfish lunatic. The only reason I wanted to "live" was because the doctors didn't cut my leg off. This meant I could still get back to playing football. All of this drama going on was a mere Cliffs Note on my road to the Pro Football Hall of Fame.

My "faith" was redeemed, hallelujah, praises to God!

See, I was just being set up for a marvelous comeback. I truly believed this garbage.

In between coming down off morphine highs and eating bowls of Cheerios, I would casually ask visiting doctors, "Be honest, how far back does this push my rehab?" They would just look at me with such dismay. I believe they felt sorry for me. They believed my career was over. They weren't even sure I was going to live. In their eyes,

I was either insane, or still hallucinating.

7 CHAPTER

QUESTIONS WITHOUT ANY ANSWERS

It wasn't until after the second debridement surgery and a few weeks into my hospital stay that some of the picture of what was going on became clearer. I began to stabilize. My white blood cell count was increasing, which was a positive sign the antibiotics were working.

There was a little less stress in the room. My mother began to ask questions. When a mama bear is on the hunt, beware. I wasn't allowed to physically leave my room, but this didn't stop my family from roaming the halls and meeting family members of other patients.

We learned that I was one of many players for the Cleveland Browns who dealt with postoperative infections. In fact, there was another player on the exact same floor that was there dealing with an infection. This seemed to be a trend. This was information I was not made aware of prior to surgery.

Hell, you can't even buy a used 1989 Honda Accord without a CarFax report revealing every fender bender the car had ever been in. Information is king when making a decision, especially one regarding your health. Well, I was weeks removed from surgery before my infection reared its ugly head.

Where did the infection come from? When this question is asked to medical professionals you better have on some boots because the bullshit is about to get thick. You will hear … bacteria are in your nose … it's on your skin … it's on your television remote … and … we live in a world full of bacteria.

This may all be true, but it means they end up saying a whole lot without saying anything. Everyone is going to cover their asses. It took legal proceedings to begin to piece together my situation.

You remember the five-millimeter tear after the first patellar tendon repair? The one when my knee jerked in the early morning as I was putting on my knee brace? That small tear is what saved my life. My infection sat dormant inside my knee for a period of time, medically referred to as the MRSA incubation period. This is when the bacteria will remain in a dormant state until it is exposed to an environment best suited for growth.

This tiny tear in the tendon resulted in some internal bleeding. A small stitch along the repaired tendon was infected. When the fresh blood pooled around the infected area, the fuse was lit, boom. But where did the infection come from? Let's just say this: Historical data can be a tremendous tool in determining future outcomes.

After eight weeks, I was ready to be discharged from the

hospital. This was a bittersweet time. The nursing staff at the Cleveland Clinic was beyond phenomenal. They treated me like family.

After spending an extended amount of time around people who witnessed me at my most vulnerable state and to have them nurse me back to a level of health, it was inevitable to feel a bond with them. I could feel their genuine empathy and concern for what I was going through. A part of the reason I was forced to stay in the hospital for such a lengthy period of time was because the doctors wanted my wound to be healed prior to leaving.

This made total sense. I had gone through six weeks of intravenous antibiotics and had been switched over to an oral antibiotic pill. My white blood cell count was trending upward. This was all positive. But there was small problem. My wound was not fully healed. There was a very small opening at the bottom of my scar, toward the top of my shin. The opening was about the half the size of an eraser at the top of a No. 2 pencil.

It just wouldn't heal.

I was given a box of wound dressings, a prescription for antibiotics, and was sent home. There's no way to describe how excited I was to leave. That excitement would be short-lived.

8 CHAPTER

WHAT DOESN'T KILL YOU…MAKES YOU AN ADDICT

We all can relate to the feeling of missing sleep in our own bed. A few nights away from the comforts of home can do us some good, sometimes. But there comes a point when home is where we need to be.

I was well beyond that mark. There was a deep need to just be alone. For weeks on end, I was bombarded with people. An often-overlooked component to mental health is balance. We need to surround ourselves with people who genuinely care about us, but it's also just as important to invest alone time into ourselves.

It was a challenge for my mother to leave me unaccompanied, considering she slept in a chair next to me every night during my stay in the Cleveland Clinic. When I was home in my bed, I had cable and some good food. But there was a problem. I couldn't sleep.

In the hospital, I had difficulty sleeping for obvious reasons, so I was prescribed Benadryl. This wasn't the familiar over-the-counter tablet form of Benadryl usually taken for allergy issues; it was a liquid that was injected directly into my PICC (peripherally inserted central catheter).

The PICC was inserted into one of the veins just below the bend of my right elbow. The tube was snaked through the vein with the end of the tube positioned near my heart. Having a PICC made administering my antibiotics easier and more effective, because the antibiotics would be more readily dispersed, as my heart would pump.

It was also used as a delivery method for my Benadryl. I'd later learn how dangerous this was. If the nightly euphoric high I experienced for weeks on end during my stay in the hospital was anywhere close to what a heroin addict experiences, I can totally understand why heroin is so addictive.

It was amazing. The longer I stayed in the hospital, the more I looked forward to bedtime. It got to the point where I'd wake up looking forward to going back to sleep.

The rush as the Benadryl was mainlined to my heart was like something I had never experienced. My heart would begin to rapidly beat, my body got very warm starting from my feet and ending at the top of my head, my pain and problems all melted away. My eyes would slowly close and for two minutes every night, I enjoyed being in the hospital.

What I didn't know was that I was slowly becoming dependent on substances to "feel" better.

The first night out of the hospital, I was up all night. There's nothing to be alarmed about, because I was just excited to be home; of course I couldn't sleep, right? Wrong. It wasn't until the second night when I decided I'd have to figure out a way to get some shut-eye. I had watched enough television. I was tired. I needed to sleep.

Part of my discharge instruction was not to drive, but there was a car in the garage and keys on the kitchen counter. I was about to roll out. It took me more time than anticipated to crutch myself to the garage and configure myself behind the wheel, but I made it.

My first and only stop, Walgreens. I crutched around the store looking for my 'solution.'

"Do you guys have liquid Benadryl?" I asked the cashier.

She looked at me as if I had two heads.

"We ain't got that. We have the tablets," she said.

Well, Benadryl is Benadryl, right? The tablets must be the same thing.

Boy was I wrong. I bought one box of extra strength and headed home. The night started off with three of the pink oval shaped tablets.

I didn't feel a thing, so I popped three more.

Still wide-awake.

I'm not ready give up just yet. Maybe I'm not taking enough? I took one more tablet, because, you know, I didn't want to overdo it.

Still nothing.

Once again, I was set to be up all night. This was before the days of Netflix and a seemingly unlimited supply of entertainment. I was bored out of my mind. You've probably heard the adage, "an idle mind is the devil's workshop." Well the devil was busy in my head.

I had an idea. Pain pills floated around NFL locker rooms like Skittles. They were never my "thing" because I didn't like how they made me feel sleepy. Hold on, did someone say sleep?

Yes, please sign me up for a double dose. There was a full bottle of Percocet in the bathroom. I quickly downed three Percocet and slowly dozed off to sleep.

This was the beginning of a problem.

9 CHAPTER

HERE WE GO AGAIN

Two weeks out of the hospital, I was slowly beginning to accept there was a long road ahead. My daily routine consisted of changing the dressing over my still-open wound, playing video games, taking antibiotics, and popping Percocet, although the Percocet were no longer a mere sleep aid.

I had reached the level of "recreational" usage. In my mind, this was nothing to be concerned about. It was all under control.

The one element that was out of my control was my scar fully healing. This damn hole just wouldn't close. It was to the point where I'd wake up in the morning to my lower leg sticking to my sheets, because oozing discharge had soaked through the knee dressing and onto my bed.

It was a thick and yellowish fluid. These episodes of oozing were not new, which was why I was discharged from the hospital with a box of bandages and instructed to change the dressing every two hours. If changing my bandages every two hours and washing sheets each morning was the tradeoff for me to not be in the hospital, then so be it. It was a small price to pay.

The doctors wanted me to come in for a scheduled follow-up appointment to see how things were shaping up. Outside of my trip to Walgreens, I hadn't been out of the house in two weeks, so I was looking forward to this appointment. I was especially excited to see the nursing staff that had taken such great care of me.

Crutches, not a wheelchair, were my preferred method of transportation. The visit began in a very positive fashion. Everyone was excited to see me, and I was happy to see them. But this excitement was about to come to a screeching halt. During the battery of preliminary diagnostic tests — blood pressure, pulse, and temperature — the medical staff discovered I had a slight fever.

In typical circumstances, a slightly elevated fever is nothing to be overly concerned about, but when the patient has been battling an infection, it's not typical. An increase in body temperature is a sign of the body fighting an infection. Although I felt fine, I was immediately readmitted to the hospital.

What in the hell just happened? Hold on, I just wanted to get checked out and go back home. Yea, the people were nice and all, but there's really good cable television at my house, that's where I want to be. It didn't matter what I thought. Within 15 minutes I had another plastic patient bracelet slapped on my wrist and was back in the exact same room I had just vacated two weeks prior. This couldn't be real.

Except it was very real. Some cultures were taken on the knee, and it was soon discovered I was still infected. But there was a new culprit that had invaded my body. The previous malefactor had been MRSA, but the new offender was an entirely new acronym: MRSE.

"So y'all are telling me I still have an infection? But I don't feel sick," I said with a strong look of confusion on my face.

See, that's the problem with MRSE versus MRSA. With MRSA, you are going to show very clear signs of something being direly wrong, but MRSE is the much more subdued but insidious cousin or MRSA. It just quietly hangs out in the shadows.

The silence of MRSE ultimately destroyed my knee. Remember, infections prevent healing while also eating away at tissue. They lead to articular cartilage degeneration (the cartilage covering the ends of bone). There will be more on this later. Here's what you need to understand right now: I was pissed. My bullshit alarm was beginning to make a slight humming sound.

But the level of pissed off I had reached was irrelevant. They were keeping me, and I ended up staying another two weeks in the hospital. These two next weeks were miserable. I just had a two-week furlough and now I'm back in medical imprisonment.

What truly had me upset was the fact I once again had zero clue as to how long I would be there. Was this going to be another eight-week bid? What if it's longer? My mind was burnt out.

While my room was the same room as before, it seemed smaller. It was as if each of the walls had moved in four feet closer to the bed.

The only bright side was Benadryl, right? Wrong.

My PICC line was out. And since my antibiotics were oral treatments, they weren't putting one back in. There was no way in hell the nurses were going to give me four or five Percocet in one dose.

This is what I had self-prescribed while on furlough. How was I going to get through this? I didn't have the answer to this question, so I chose silence. There aren't many people who will describe me as talkative, but this was another level of silence. There was nothing for me to talk about.

I wanted answers and couldn't get them. Doctors were beginning to be very cagey with what they said. I hadn't spoken with anyone inside of the organization other than a brief phone call with then head coach Romeo Crennel.

Articles began to slowly pop up that my "career was over," but they completely failed to mention I nearly died from an infection.

Who's saying this stuff? Where did that information come from? Something just didn't feel right.

Fine, if this was where my life was, I was perfectly content with riding the wave until it settled softly along the shores of

Lake Erie or crashed into the jagged rocks littered along the lake's breakwall.

It didn't matter to me.

10 CHAPTER

HANGING WITH THE GERIATRICS CREW

OK, let's try this again.

I was discharged from the Cleveland Clinic for the second time after a two-week stay. Once again, all signs pointed toward me being "free of infection." But the one key sign overlooked was that pesky hole in my scar that was not healing.

The doctors said it would "heal in time."

All right, if time is what it would take, time is what I had to give. I just knew that time could no longer be spent in a hospital. My instincts were whispering to me something wasn't quite right, but I knew that time would surely reveal the truth.

I was correct.

Once out of the hospital, I was slated to begin light physical therapy. This was the mental shift I was craving. My mind and body didn't feel the same. Getting myself back moving and working on feeling better was better than any medication the doctors could have prescribed. The only "strange" part of my physical therapy regimen was I wouldn't be inside the Browns facility and a person I had never met would be in charge of my rehabilitation.

Trust me, I wasn't too keen on being back in the Browns facility anyway. I was a mess, and my vanity wouldn't allow me to be seen in this light. I felt it was a little weird to be rehabbing with what I called the "geriatrics crew," but I didn't mind.

Most of the other patients were older people rehabbing from an array of orthopedic issues. They didn't know who the hell I was and didn't seem to care. It was strange, but perfect at the time.

My physical therapist was a really good man. Strangely, I felt a little sorry for him, because I knew what I was dealing with was completely over his head. My knee looked like a mafia hit had been called on it.

There was no protocol for what he was dealing with, and most importantly, the entire Browns medical staff was beginning to faction off to their respective ass-covering positions. This man had no clue to the hornet's nest he was dumped into. Nevertheless, he was a consummate professional.

This time abruptly ended when I crutched myself into rehab like I had a jet pack attached to my ass. To my dismay, I had awakened that morning to find a white string hanging out of the hole in my leg. If you get queasy from envisioning gross things, grab yourself a barf bucket.

I sat up in the bed as I did every morning and did my morning knee check.

"Did the hole heal, yet?" I would ask myself as I inspected the wound.

This morning was different. Initially, I thought the white thread was dried discharge. Then my mind went to some horror movie shit.

"Was that a maggot?" I thought to myself.

No, it wasn't a maggot, thank God! I would have probably sawed my leg off with a butter knife had it been. I reached down to physically inspect what in the hell this was. I grabbed and gently pinched the thread between my thumb and pointer finger and slowly began to peel it from my skin.

"Oh this is just a piece of string from the sheets," I thought to myself.

As the thread slowly peeled away from the skin and I began to lift the thread, my flesh began to slowly rise with it, and I felt a gentle tug from *inside* my knee.

"What the fuck is this?" I said out loud as if anyone could hear me.

I panicked and let go of the thread.

Hold on, this thread seems to be attached to something on the inside of my body. Let me be sure. It's early in the morning and maybe my eyes are deceiving me.

I reached back toward the thread and tugged at it again. I will never forget the unsettling feeling inside my knee. It felt as if there was a steak knife inside the knee that was poking its way out. My mind and body started moving at warp speed. Within minutes I was cleaned up, dressed, and crutching my way into the Cleveland Clinic.

"Hey, is doc here today? I need to see him, now!" I said to the therapist in reference to the head team surgeon.

The therapist sensed something was wrong.

"What do you need? Can I help?" he said with complete sincerity.

"Hell no. Get doc right now." I said.

You remember that slight humming sound my "bullshit meter" was emitting a little while back? Well it was full alarm now.

The team doctor eventually found his way to me. We walked into a private office. I sat on the table and positioned my leg to reveal what I had just discovered.

"Doc, what the hell is this?" I said pointing to the thread.

Without any sign of panic he said, "That's one of the sutures from the tendon repair."

He then pulled scissors out of his pocket, pulled the thread in an upward fashion, and cut it.

You remember my "bullshit meter that was at full alarm? Well, it was now screaming at DEFCON level 5.

"What the fuck just happened?" I thought to myself. "There

was no way that was sanitary."

It was time for me to get away from these people.

11 CHAPTER

SCREW THIS, I'M OUTTA HERE

I booked a flight to Birmingham, Alabama, that afternoon for the next morning. My financial adviser happened to live in Fairhope, Alabama, and was able to use some of his established contacts to get me in for a visit with Dr. James Andrews the next afternoon.

If you don't know James Andrews, he's basically the Bruce Springsteen of the orthopedic community. He's a medical rock star. If there was anyone who could help me begin to piece together what was going on, he was as good a person to start as anyone in the world. But it would instead be his nursing assistant who would make quite a stirring revelation.

As I sat on the waiting table to see Dr. Andrews, his nursing assistant came in to go over some preliminary paperwork. She took a look at my knee and said in the most delicate Southern accent, "Oh, you got an infection; gotta get that cleaned up."

My heart sank.

I had just sat in Cleveland with some of the most "prestigious" medical professionals in the world, and a nursing assistant told me after one look that I had an infection when these other people who saw me nearly every day for weeks said I was "fine."

Shortly after, the boss confirmed the diagnosis and determined I needed another surgical procedure to save my leg. Yes, amputation again was possible. Cultures were taken and sent to the lab, but apparently we weren't trying to find a needle in a haystack. The problem was staring us all in the face, or at least some of us.

"Well, can you fix it?" I asked.

I didn't get the answer I was hoping for. Andrews advised me to go back to Cleveland and let the medical staff get this back on track. That was not going to happen. My trust was gone; anger had taken over. There were so many questions I needed to get answered, but I first had to get this knee fixed, or lose my leg.

I made a call to my agents who were based in New York. They had a great relationship with the Giants team surgeon, Dr. Russ Warren. I flew from Birmingham that afternoon directly to New York City. The next morning, I was in Dr. Warren's office.

Dr. Warren wasn't a rock star. He was a quiet legend. While some doctors reach a level of accreditation that surpasses their capabilities, this guy was a true genius who performed some of the most difficult and innovative procedures that have ever been performed in this country. And I was hoping like hell he could help me.

His nurse strolled into the waiting room to gather all of the pertinent details so she could properly present a macro-level understanding of my situation to Dr. Warren. She asked to take a look at my knee. I nervously fumbled to get myself situated on the table. She tilted her head down to glance over the top rim of her glasses and said, "Oh, we are dealing with an infection. I will get some cultures so we can know exactly what kind."

This isn't happening, I said to myself. When am I going to wake up from this damn nightmare? Why is this happening to me? I wanted so badly to feel sorry for myself, but anger was all I could muster. But this wasn't the time to be angry. I needed to think as clearly as possible.

I wasn't going to be leaving New York City for a while. Dr. Warren scheduled me for surgery the following day. The concern at the time was saving my limb. The infection had destroyed my skin and joint. The texture of my knee was similar to a wet sponge. It was a fluid-filled ball of mush. The integrity of what we know a knee to be was not there.

I underwent another debridement procedure to clean out as much of the infected tissue as possible. Another PICC was inserted in my opposite arm to begin intravenous antibiotics for another six weeks. The plan was for me to spend six weeks in the Hospital for Special Surgery in New York City.

The irony. My room was in a wing of the hospital dedicated to Randy Lerner, the then-owner of the Cleveland Browns. At this point, God was just poking at me.

I was in the hospital for two weeks. Things were going as well as they could. Then one day I had a special visitor: Randy Lerner, the team owner.

I won't lie; it felt good to have him stop to check on me. Although my relationship with the organization was quickly eroding, I had a unique affinity for Randy Lerner.

You have to understand that it was my dream to be a Cleveland Brown. When free agency began, the Cleveland Browns didn't have any interest in me. It wasn't because they didn't like me as a player; it was because they weren't a good team and needed to fill so many other key positions that a center was the last thing they were concerned about. An elite center at the time was equivalent to placing a delicious cherry on top of a spoiled milkshake. It didn't make sense to them.

But that didn't matter to me. I gave my agent very clear marching orders: Get me to Cleveland or don't call me again.

So they had to create interest where there was none. This is nearly impossible, because it goes against the very nature of how free agency works. When you are the prettiest girl at the dance, all the boys want to dance with you. I was the prettiest girl at the dance, but Johnny didn't want to be my dance partner. I had to be resourceful.

There was one person I knew had the political cache to help me land in The Land: Jim Tressel, former legendary Ohio State football head coach. I placed a call to coach Tressel to see if he could use his vast network of contacts to assist in making my dream come true. In typical Tressel fashion, he got it done.

When Jim Tressel calls, people answer the phone; this includes billionaire NFL team owners. When the team owner decides he wants something, he gets what he wants. Shortly before the start of free agency, the Browns executives called my agents to let them know "we are in." And just like that, the Browns pursuit of me in free agency was no longer a football decision, but a business one.

This is why the first thing I did after signing my contract in Cleveland was to seek out Randy Lerner to ask for *his* autograph. He grabbed a Browns helmet that was resting on his desk, signed it, "LeCharles – Welcome Home – Randy Lerner – 2006 Go Browns." This helmet still proudly sits in my home library, and it's never going anywhere.

12 CHAPTER

THE ORIGINAL "FAKE NEWS"

At this point on the calendar, my scheduled six-week stay in New York City would have taken me through Thanksgiving and Christmas. There was no way I was spending these holidays alone in Manhattan. My agent brought me some of the best-tasting food the New York delis had to offer, but there's nothing like the comforts of home during the holidays.

After extensive begging on my end and some strategic planning on the hospital's side, they were going to let me go home. The principal concern was the administration of my intravenous antibiotics. Where would I get the medicine? Who would administer it? Who was going to become my primary care provider?

I didn't have all of the answers but there was a consensus that I was not going back to the Cleveland Clinic or to the care of the Browns medical staff. The adage "where there's a will, there's a way" was in full effect.

A plan was devised for me to be transferred to the care of University Hospitals in Cleveland. Their lead infectious disease specialist was one of the best in the country. I couldn't help but feel there was a missed opportunity considering one of the leading infectious disease specialists was down the street from the very room I stayed in at the Cleveland Clinic.

My intravenous antibiotics would be prescribed by him and delivered each morning to my home in a cooler. I had become very proficient in managing the administration of my antibiotics. Clearly I had seen it done enough times. Unwrap all of the IV tubing, close the valve on the tubing, gently push the tubing spike into the IV bag's port, hang the IV pouch of Vancomycin on to the IV stand, be sure to not let the tip of the tubing touch the ground, lightly squeeze the tubing's drip-chamber to fill it about half way with the liquid, position the end of the IV tube over a plastic cup, then open the valve to fill the hose with Vancomycin, close the valve, double check to be sure there are no air bubbles in the line, attach the tubing to the port of my PICC, open the valve, then start playing video games for the next hour while gravity did its job.

See, it was simple.

I'd repeat this pattern three times a day, every four hours. The next four weeks were spent sitting in my basement, administering antibiotics, playing video games and taking pain pills. It was a miserable time, but at least I wasn't in the hospital.

My patience was wearing thin. My body was a shell of itself. My mind was in a dark place. The last five months had been the most trying time of my life, but at the same time the most forging, strengthening.

I had no idea where the road in front of me was going. But I was sure Cleveland wasn't the best place for me at that moment. This feeling wasn't a desire to be traded or released from the Browns. My sentiment was toward the city of Cleveland. This wasn't about football; this was about me wanting to leave the city that raised me, my home. Cleveland had become toxic for my mind. There was a narrative being painted about me that wasn't close to being the truth.

The reporting about me was indeed "fake news" before fake news was even fake news. I knew there were people inside the organization who were intentionally creating a false storyline to avoid acknowledging gross negligent patterns that plagued the organization.

Therefore, I was made out to be the bad guy. It was made to appear that I was exhibiting reclusive behavior and not wanting to be a part of the organization.

"But I nearly died, nobody is going to discuss this?" I silently asked myself.

There were instances where my true intentions in wanting to be a Cleveland Brown were doubted.

"Now my decency as a man is up for debate?" I rhetorically questioned to myself.

Some were saying I only came to Cleveland to "steal money."

"Damn, my integrity is being contested," I thought.

It was news to me, but apparently I had torn my patellar tendon playing basketball and faked as if the injury happened in practice.

The grumblings ranged from sinister to the nonsensical. What hurt the most was fans were beginning to believe this rubbish. It was one thing for the Browns executives to play the politics game, but to see media members I grew up watching on television and reading proliferate the trash they were fed by the team hurt in a manner that I wasn't emotionally prepared for.

Fans were openly saying they didn't want me back. I was a waste of money. I was a fraud. They were ready to move on. The Browns' spin machine was working.

I was crushed. This wasn't the Cleveland I knew. True Clevelanders are loyal. True Clevelanders can't be fed soup with a fork; they smell bullshit from a mile away. But this was a different time in Cleveland.

The city was desperate to be relevant and any shiny nickel that rolled into town with promises of "turning around" the organization would be granted messiah status without ever having to earn it. You remember, "In Phil we trust," the statement about the general manager who signed me? I sure do. The city was clinging to its last bit of dignity and if this meant one of their own had to be thrown overboard to save the ship, so be it.

This wasn't the Cleveland I loved. It was different. It was time for me to go.

13 CHAPTER

THE DESERT BECAME MY HOME

The scope of places I called "home" was limited to Cleveland, Columbus, and New Orleans. Where in the hell was I going to go?

My agent had a great relationship with a physical therapist by the name of Brett Fischer in Phoenix, Arizona. I had met Brett as a player and worked with him on some hip mobility during a previous offseason. Brett was a great person and smart.

My antibiotics had once again been reduced to an oral tablet, and Dr. Warren cleared me to begin physical therapy. The plan was to spend about four months working to break down scar tissue to regain full range of motion in the knee joint. My leg had been locked at "zero" for months, meaning it was immobilized in a straight position. The scar tissue was so severe that my leg could not bend, at all. My limb was rigid like a piece of 2x4 lumber and about the same size as one.

Dr. Warren's plan was for me to get as far removed from the complications of the infections as possible, regain mobility, and establish a baseline level of function prior to him redoing the entire patellar tendon surgery. I would be starting all over from square one in four months. The next four months would in essence be "pre-habilitation" to prepare me for the upcoming surgery.

Well, Brett was a great physical therapist, I needed to begin therapy, and Arizona wasn't cold like Cleveland. I was headed to the Southwest.

My home-buying process was unorthodox to say the least. I packed one bag and flew to Arizona on a Monday with my brother. A Realtor named Randy Bos met us at Phoenix Sky Harbor Airport and our home search began. Randy had a list of potential places.

I wasn't looking for an extravagant mansion. I just needed a modest location where I could entrench myself for this journey. The plane landed at 11 a.m. and by 12:30 p.m. we had found the house. I wrote a check for the total cost and signed the paperwork. Tuesday morning I was directing furniture movers on where to place what.

It was time for me to get my shit together.

I was back. Yes, my body was broken, but my spirit was on the rise. For months I was not in control of my day-to-day existence. This was well outside the wheelhouse I had grown accustomed. You can't possibly name a high-level achiever in any profession who is not a control freak. I don't mean "control freak" in the context of someone who manipulates others to exert power over them. Those people are just insecure assholes. A person who has attained extraordinary success is a master at controlling areas of their life that directly affects their achievement.

My hands had been taken off the steering wheel, but now I was back driving. The picture was clearing. I was going to crush the next four months, but my mind wouldn't allow me to rehab as if I was going in to another surgery.

Although this was the case, I don't believe it's possible to be your best when operating under a self-limiting mindset. Nobody is going to use the best materials to build a house they are planning to tear down. I wasn't merely "pre-habbing." Pre-habilitation is for losers. I was training.

This all sounds real badass, right? Yes, I was back being "badass Bentley." But don't you remember when Mr. Badass had his faith tested in the most arduous fashion? And he flunked.

"Hold on, LeCharles, don't start this shit again," I thought to myself on those quiet nights sitting alone. The Lord has carried me my entire life, and the very moment He needed me to be steadfast in my faith. I flinched.

Yea, I was physically and mentally strong, but my faith was weak. I couldn't fall back into the trap I had just come from. I had been spiritually exposed and there was no way I could just overlook it.

This entire experience was a test of my faith, not strength. God will never burden us with more than we can handle, correct?

This is wrong. It sounds good, but it's just not the truth. God *has* to give us more than we can handle so we can see just how truly weak we are without Him. Think about faith strengthening in the context of weight training. In order to increase muscular strength and size, we have to stress our muscles by lifting increasingly heavier loads than we believe we are capable of lifting.

What happens?

The muscle tissues are torn, and then heal over time to become stronger and bigger. If we keep lifting the same weights, we don't get stronger.

It's the same phenomenon with our faith. You will be given more than you can handle, and you will fail. But it is only "failure" when we don't recognize our "failure" as truly an opportunity to get stronger. We must then keep repeating this cycle so we can eventually manage larger and larger faith-testing circumstances.

When you fail during your last rep on a bench press, do you never go back to the gym? Of course you do. I failed my big test, but I was about to bounce back stronger than ever.

14 CHAPTER

HEALTH IS WEALTH

My first mission was to begin breaking down scar tissue that had taken over my knee joint.

At times the pain was unbearable. The method wasn't passive. It was literally a hands-on approach of manually manipulating the knee joint to mobilize it.

Each morning was a declared war on what my body had created to protect itself. There were some days where zero progress would be made. On other days I would feel a big "pop" inside my knee and suddenly there would be two more degrees of flexion. I remember lying on the therapy table drenched in sweat as if I had just completed a full workout in the Phoenix sun, but I hadn't moved from the table. The process was intense and grueling.

I never wanted anyone inside of the therapy center to see the level of discomfort I was in. My fear was they'd dial back on my therapy. I wanted to push onward, so I would take three or four Percocet in the morning just to get me through 90 minutes of therapy.

With any type of drug we ingest over an extended period of

time, our body begins to need more of it to elicit the ideal effect. The three or four in the morning turned into five or six.

When the pain of wrenching my knee earlier that day would take hold in the evening hours, I would need another five or six to get me through the night.

But my body wasn't in a state to process so much poison. I had just completed 12 weeks of one of the world's most potent antibiotics, Vancomycin, which can be extremely harsh on the liver and kidneys. My kidneys had been under so much distress that for a few weeks following the last surgery, my urine was tinted to a pinkish hue, because there was blood in it.

The last four months had consisted of anesthesia (three surgeries), two six-week Vancomycin cycles, weeks of oral antibiotics, two months of Benadryl pushes, countless pain pills, and multiple refilled prescriptions of anti-inflammatories.

My body's toxic load had surpassed a manageable threshold. The additional stress of managing the toxicity of pain pills caused a harsh reaction.

I would get unbearably nauseous after consuming the pills. The kind of nausea that caused me to sit with a garbage can tucked under my chin for hours, sweating, dry heaving, and drooling from my mouth praying to throw up.

But I couldn't. It didn't take long to decide that if I was going to make these next four months count, I had to find a better way to manage my pain.

When I was growing up, my father constantly preached the importance of taking care of my health. He never missed an opportunity to remind me "health is wealth."

It wasn't mere lip service. This was a man who led by example. My father was 58 when I was born, yet throughout my childhood and even up until his death at 86 I never saw my dad as an "old man." He was always so strong, active and healthy.

The value of health was instilled in me at an early age. This appreciation had a tremendous impact on my development as an athlete. I generally ate better and trained harder than my peers at every level. But I was now in a place where I had to truly lean on my health-conscious upbringing to pull myself out of a deficit in my well-being.

Ever see those weird people meandering through the grocery store aisles reading the labels on every item they pick up? Yea, I became one of those people. If the product didn't say "natural" or "organic," I didn't buy it. Yes, looking back on it, I now understand more thoroughly how misleading those monikers can be.

My goal was to focus on foods that were nature's version of anti-inflammatories. I began to move away from wheat, sugar, dairy, Omega-6 fats, and starchy foods in general. There was a significant increase in my intake of Omega-3 fats, nuts, garlic, turmeric, cinnamon, cayenne, avocado, and cherries.

I set up a meal-delivery plan that would drop off three meals a day to my front door. My plan was to eat five meals every day. This forced me to cook for myself. I began viewing my food selection as an extension of my recovery; I wanted to play an active role in the healing process.

It's so easy to slip into a mindset of dependency when our health falters. I'd watch people every day come to therapy, lie on the table, and act like a dead fish for 45 minutes. They were not mentally engaged in the process.

Doctors and therapists aren't magicians. They are the navigators in our recovery, but we captain the ship. Our minds play a significant role in our recovery and long-term well-being. But we must train ourselves to tap into our inherent healing potential.

Connecting the body and mind is made out to require some sort of out-of-body experience. This isn't true. The first step in doing so is to simply pay attention to how you feel.

My father would often greet me with a stern, "Take account of yourself." It was his country way of asking, "How are you doing?"

I've adopted a similar investigative tactic with my kids. Each morning they are going to get two questions from me, "How did you sleep?" and "How do you feel?"

Similar to my father, I'm not looking for a dissertation in response. I ask these questions for two reasons: because I'm concerned for their welfare, and I want them to be in the habit of staying in tune with themselves. Our lives can become so inundated with external diversions such as work, social media, relationships, finances, and our fantasy football draft picks that we forget how to connect with ourselves. We wind up spending more time "liking" the snapshots of other people's lives, than we do actually "liking" ourselves.

Getting refocused on my nutrition and engaging in my healing process brought balance back to my body and spirit.

15 CHAPTER

RIDING A BIKE AIN'T SO EASY

It took about eight weeks, but a big day had finally arrived. I was able to make a full revolution on the stationary bike.

Some of you may be thinking, it took eight weeks to pedal a bike? Yes, it took eight full weeks to get just one complete turn of the pedals.

Riding a stationary bike became the go-to method to help break down the scar tissue. There was only so much manual therapy that could be done. When someone else is cranking on your knee, it's difficult for the therapist to measure how much pressure is too much pressure.

The procedure for increasing the range of motion in the knee joint went like this: I would sit on the edge of the therapy table with a densely rolled towel or a thick wooden dowel positioned toward the bottom of my hamstring. Either of the two would serve as a fulcrum. The therapist would then place one hand on my thigh and the other hand on my shinbone. Now envision the pumping action of drawing water from a well pump and that about sums up the method. The more range of motion we gained, the more difficult and painful the routine became.

There was concern for a potential lower limb fracture that was increasing by the day, thus the stationary bike became a safer option. A stationary bike gave me more control of the process. When I reached a sticking point while pedaling, I'd reverse the pedals and slowly rock the pedals back and forth until there was a breakthrough. Some breakthroughs took longer than others, but it was all part of the process. I felt myself getting closer to completing a full cycle, and then it happened.

On the big day, my therapist and others had gathered because they all knew the significance of the milestone. I had gone through my preliminary warm-up for the day that consisted of a heat pack, ultrasound, manual massage, and leg lifts.

I couldn't wait to get on the bike. It was my day. I felt it.

The pedaling began with slow back-and-forth rocking movements. I'd slowly go forward and then slowly backward. It didn't matter how much range of motion I had ended with the day before, I had to slowly re-establish that range of motion prior to setting a new mark.

Some days I wouldn't get back to the prior day's mark because of either swelling or soreness. This would cause me some frustration with the process. But I felt good about that particular day.

I was 20 minutes in, and then, boom; I hit my old sticking point.

I was 30 minutes in, and then boom; I surpassed the new benchmark.

But I was still a little bit away from the full turn. Both pedals were in full north and south positions. I was so tempted to cheat by slightly lifting my left hip off the bike seat. This would give me a little extra room to get the complete turnover.

Screw that, I was too close.

My high school offensive line coach, Marty Eynon, used to always tell me, "The closer you get to your goal, the harder you'll need to work." I lived by that.

I was 45 minutes in, and then, boom, the pedals completely turned over. By this time there was a significant crowd gathered around me that I hadn't noticed. The therapy center sort of took on the structure of a group support system where everybody cheered on the milestones of the next person. Everyone was clapping and cheering.

I felt so proud of myself and appreciative of the support I was given by Brett Fischer and his staff. I gathered enough strength to pull my sweat-drenched body off the bike and onto a therapy table where ice and compression would be applied.

As I lay on the table, the events of the last seven months were racing through my head. Seven months prior to that day, I wanted to die. There I was seven months later feeling more alive than I ever had in my life.

This is the irony of life. Today may be dark, but we can only discover the brightness of tomorrow by living through today's darkness. It may not be fair, but it's life. And life is a beautiful thing when we commit ourselves to living it.

Over the next four months I would have two follow-up visits with Dr. Warren. My progress was right on track, but I had to complete the third and final examination prior to setting the date for the complete overhaul of my patellar tendon operation.

All of the signs were pointing toward the third examination being a smashing success. I was excited and feeling good. The key benchmarks that would determine when the next procedure would take place were regained joint mobility and muscle tone in my left quad.

Well, the joint was back operating through a full range of motion, and there were even signs of muscle beginning to wake up from hibernation. The four months in Phoenix were a challenge, but I was so thrilled about finally taking positive steps toward getting back my life and career back on track.

It was time for me to head back to New York City.

16 CHAPTER

GO BUY A BOAT AND FISH

It was mild spring day in April of 2007 when I would be confronted with the reality I was probably never going to play football again.

I eagerly marched into Dr. Warren's office for my third and final checkup appointment. You remember the excitement you had as a child when you'd be sitting in class and the teacher would ask a question and you knew the answer? You'd shoot your arm into the sky like a bottle rocket on the Fourth of July waiting for her to call on you?

Yea, that's how I felt as I waited for Dr. Warren to enter the examination room. I just knew he was going to be impressed with my progress.

What I didn't know was the extent to which he would be impressed. As he assertively manipulated my leg to evaluate the flexibility of my hamstrings, range of motion in the joint, and muscle density of the quadriceps, I sat there with a snarky grin, thinking to myself, "Yea, this is pretty cool, I did it."

It took about two minutes for him to complete the full examination. I used to think to myself once my previous appointments had been completed, "I flew all the way from Arizona for this man to see me for two minutes."

But this was part of the process. I understood that. My expectations for this visit were for him to tell me how awesome I was progressing, which he did.

My expectations for this visit were for him to gladly schedule my next surgery, which he did not.

"LeCharles, you have done a great job. This has come along better than I anticipated," he said.

I was smiling like a kid on Christmas morning.

"Ok, so when do you want to operate?" I asked.

Dr. Warren then folded his arms, looked directly in to my eyes and said, "I'm not."

My heart felt like it had dropped in to my stomach.

"What do you mean?" I asked.

"You're doing great. I can't risk your life by performing another tendon surgery on you. There's a chance for a spore of MRSA to be dormant in the joint, and if I put a cadaver tendon in your knee, and that tendon becomes infected, there's a very good chance you won't live," he said.

My head slumped toward the floor.

"How can I play football again?" I murmured.

"Look, you're never playing football again. You'll be lucky to walk without a limp the rest of your life," he said.

I raised my head and looked at him and asked, "So, what should I do?"

His infamous words to me were, "Go buy a boat and fish."

With those words, he shook my hand and walked out of the door. The examination was over.

My emotions had been on such a roller coaster ride the last nine months that I had become emotionless in relation to the "news" that was delivered to me. The bad news was no longer bad news. The good news was always seasoned with a pessimistic grain of salt. My mind had become embedded in *the process*.

See, here's the secret to success within the process many people don't understand. The process is willing to account for emotion, but it can't account for the emotional.

I had been emotional early in this journey, and it prevented me from seeing the bigger picture. By not being emotional, I was able to greatly appreciate the words uttered by Dr. Warren.

They may not have been the words I *wanted* to hear, but they were the words I *needed* to hear.

For months I had questions that were unanswered. And if they were answered in many instances they were disingenuous company lines that skirted the truth.

Dr. Warren had told me the truth. It may have been delivered in a stoic and cold fashion, but we are talking about a man who at that time had been practicing medicine longer than I had been alive. This wasn't the first time he had to be the bearer of bad news. There was nothing I could have done differently to change the outcome.

I left his office with a very clear mind.

In fact, reflecting back on it, I now realize he knew all along he wouldn't be performing the surgery. But had he told me that four months prior there was a very good chance I would not have made the progress I did, when I believed my training was genuine preparation for another surgery. It was a brilliant tactical move on his end. But he overlooked one crucial aspect.

I was a city kid from Cleveland who hated boats. I wasn't ready to concede defeat.

On the plane ride back to Arizona I concocted what I thought was a brilliant plan. Of course "brilliant" is relative to the circumstances.

I was desperate. Considering my limited scope of possibilities, even the dumbest ideas sounded great at the time.

My interpretation of the conversation I had with Dr. Warren was that I was doing well and therefore he didn't see the need to operate.

OK, in his expert medical opinion, this made perfect sense; because he believed even with the surgery my football career was over.

The risk didn't outweigh the reward.

But in my non-expert medical opinion, I didn't believe my career was over, so I held on to the notion that the surgery was the best chance for me to play again.

The reward was worth the risk.

This meant I had two options. The first was to find another doctor to perform the surgery. I was crazy but not completely off my rocker. There was no way I was going to allow some hack of an orthopedic surgeon butcher me like a Christmas pig.

The second option was to train so hard the few miniscule fibers that were holding my knee together would eventually fail.

My worst-case scenario was for me to make my knee break down, and then he'd have to fix it. The best-case scenario was for the knee to adapt to the stress.

This would mean I could possibly progress enough to play again. The only thing I had to do was train as hard as possible right away, so if there were to be a significant structural failure, I could have the surgery sooner than later.

I didn't want to invest months into this kamikaze mission to have my parachute accidentally open 100 feet above the ground, land safely, and then die an hour later from an exploding landmine. Either my knee was going to explode in the middle of training, or I was going to take what I had and make it functional enough to get me back on the field.

I wasn't buying a damn boat.

Back in Arizona I was ready to go to work. Brett Fischer and I had a post examination follow up meeting so I could update him on what had transpired in New York. I explained Dr. Warren's position and then revealed to him my grand plan.

Needless to say, Brett didn't exactly see the ambitious vision I had created. He was empathetic toward my plight, but he was a medical professional. When a world-class surgeon like Dr. Warren says the sky is blue, well, the sky is more than likely going to appear blue to everyone else.

Brett was thinking like a medical expert and business owner. There was just too much risk involved for him to see my vision. Being a business owner today, I totally understand the position he had to take. I was willing to risk being injured in training. His job was to prevent people from being injured while inside his facility. This meant all "high risk" movements were off limits for me.

Well, it was going to require being engaged in "high risk" movements such as squatting, jumping, and pushing on heavy objects for me to at least see if my goal of playing was viable. I enjoyed riding the stationary bike, but that wasn't going to be enough to take me to where I wanted to go.

Brett wanted me to stay at his facility and continue to build on the progress we had made so my overall quality of life could be increased. Brett Fischer is one of the best human beings walking the face of this earth. He considered what he felt was in the best interest of my quality of life at heart. But I didn't give a damn about my "quality of life."

I wanted to play football. Consequently, I knew it was time

for me to leave Brett and find someone willing to take a gamble on helping me realize the vision I had created for myself.

I've always been blessed to have a solid network of people I could rely on. My father used to always tell me, "One shall not stand alone." He'd often utter these words when I would ask for a dollar, but he'd then instead give me two dollars. I understood the true significance of the message.

Surrounding myself with a lot of people was never high on my list of priorities. In fact, some who have known me for many years wouldn't exactly classify me as "social." But what my social network lacked in quantity was surely made up in quality. There were great people who played key roles in my success.

Now was the time for me to reclaim many of my social roots in order to keep my dream alive.

My first phone call was to Arnold Coleman. Arnold was someone who truly knew me as a person and athlete. The last eight years he had played the roles of mentor, friend, advocate and personal trainer in my life.

I met Arnold after the spring of my sophomore year in college, and he quickly became someone I trusted to help me achieve my goals. Two of those goals at the time were to break in to the Ohio State starting lineup and become a future first-round selection in the NFL Draft.

It's fair to wonder why I'd seek help outside the team when a football program like Ohio State provides players the finest resources available to be successful. I had access to the best weight room money could buy, a great strength staff, some of the best position coaches in the country, and a meal program that didn't exactly resemble "college food."

A lineage of former Buckeyes utilized the identical resources to achieve the exact same or similar goals as I had. But I saw those guys who had come before me as exceptions to the rule, not the rule.

I've always felt I had to work harder and do more than everyone else around me just to give myself a chance to compete. Much of this sentiment was homegrown; other elements were social influence.

Both my mother and father were beacons in my life of hard work and discipline. My father had a second-grade education, was raised by his grandmother whom was an emancipated slave, lied about his age to join the military at 16, survived the WWII attack on Normandy beach, and died owning two homes he paid for with cash.

He didn't know how to do anything but work.

That mindset was passed to me, which was a blessing because I wasn't always the genetic thoroughbred in the race. This is why I was the very last scholarship offer made in my recruiting class and some coaches on the staff had told me I would never play at Ohio State.

Now you understand why I could never see myself as the exception. I only saw myself as the rule, and those of us that are the "rules" must do more and be more than everyone else.

Were there things I was "exceptional" at? Absolutely. But I believe being exceptional is a birthright for some, and an earned right for others.

It wasn't a complete birthright for me, which is why I privately trained with Arnold Coleman three times a week throughout my last three seasons at Ohio State, after all of my team-mandated training. This man knew how to get the most out of me, and I needed him to work his magic once again.

Arnold Coleman wasn't just some meathead who knew his way around a gym. He is one of the most accomplished power lifters ever. And if you know anything about lifting heavy weights or just moving a heavy desk across the room, you know there's a certain mental disposition required.

It was this mental makeup that I found so intriguing about Arnold. He and I connected on a psychological level. From the first day we met, he quickly surmised that I wasn't the type of person who was easily impressed. He never attempted to "put on airs" around me. He certainly could have done so, considering how highly decorated he was in his profession. Instead, he proposed a question in our initial meeting that struck me: "Do you know what it takes to be great?"

I replied with the generic, run-of-the-mill answers many of us would typically give.

"Yea, hard work, commitment, and sacrifice," I said matter-of-factly.

"That's all true, but what if everyone was just as committed as you, or worked as hard, and sacrificed just as much?" he asked.

I had a dumbfounded look on my face, because I truly didn't have an answer. He pressed further.

"And wouldn't everyone give those same answers?"

I thought for a second.

"yea they would," I answered.

"If everyone has the same answer, then why aren't more people successful in accomplishing their goals?" he asked.

I sat down on a weight bench to process what had been thrown at me. Arnold abruptly interrupted my train of thought with the answer I was desperately seeking.

"Successful people know words don't get things done. The mind does," he said.

I looked up at Arnold as if he had just told me where Jimmy Hoffa was buried. It made so much sense. This simple concept is what propelled Arnold to the heights he had reached in his profession. It was also why he was able to "push my buttons" to get me to do things I either didn't feel like doing or thought I couldn't do.

Being exposed this early in my athletic development to such an elite level of thinking was invaluable. Arnold was in the trenches. He was busy breaking world powerlifting records. There was a tangible depth of human accomplishment acquired through his experience. See, powerlifting is similar to how tennis and golf are individual sports where success or failure is solely dependent upon the competing athlete.

There's a deeper need for the athlete to connect the body with the mind.

In the world of football, it's much easier for individuals with inferior mindsets to hide because other elite minded teammates can compensate for their shortcomings. Arnold taught me how to mentally challenge myself in ways that I had never learned in a team football environment.

Less than a week after hearing Dr. Warren's boat suggestion, I walked into the gym in Columbus, Ohio, a physical and mental shell of my former myself.

"You ready to get to work?" Arnold asked.

I looked around for the therapy table. There was nothing but weights in sight.

"Yea, what should I do to warm-up?"

He pointed to a squat rack with a 45-pound Olympic bar neatly placed at the appropriate height. I had just got pretty decent at riding a stationary bike, and this man wanted me to squat on my first day of training. I thought he was nuts, but I trusted him.

"Look, you're dead to the NFL. If we are going to do this, then let's do it," he said as he turned to walk toward the squat rack. Just like that, the fuse in my mind had been lit.

I walked directly to the squat rack and placed my right hand on the bar. So many thoughts were racing through my head, but I was overtaken by pure joy. It felt so good to be back in weight room. The metal knurling along the bar had never felt so good. I slowly glided my hand over the bar.

"Well, here we go," I said softly as I positioned myself under the bar.

I stood up to unrack the bar and took one step backward to begin my first descent. Arnold had positioned himself directly behind me and lightly placed both hands on my hips to guide me. I took a deep breath and sank into my first rep.

It was ugly but felt so damn good.

"Nice job, let's hit another one," Arnold said.

I sank into my second rep; this one was a little deeper and cleaner.

"Ok, I didn't fall apart, this is good," I thought to myself.

We completed five sets of twelve reps, and it felt like I had climbed Mt. Everest.

The workout was as emotionally draining as it was physically. It was surreal to be back in a weight room considering all of what had transpired over that last nine months.

I was finally back in my element.

17 CHAPTER

RECAPTURING MY SPIRIT

My eight weeks in Columbus would be divided between training in the morning with Arnold and pool workouts at the Ohio State football building in the afternoon. Ohio State had a treadmill that was underwater. This would allow me to work on running mechanics while unloading my bodyweight. It was a huge tool to have access to at the time.

Being able to train as hard as I wanted to while having access to Ohio State's world-class training staff and rehabilitation equipment was the best of both worlds.

I was on my own. I had zero communication with the Browns organization for six months. Once I made the decision to leave Arizona, there was no designed "medical protocol" for me to follow. My instincts were my guiding light, and it was the best thing for me.

Medically speaking, the vision I had created was impossible, thus every traditional "medical professional" I had come across didn't want to be involved with such a high-risk venture. But I was naïve enough to bet on myself when other people had long ago cashed in the chips on my career.

In eight weeks, I went from barely squatting with an Olympic bar that weighed 45 pounds to squatting 525 pounds and completely recapturing my spirit.

My time in Columbus was more mental therapy than it was physical. As my mind healed, my body would get stronger. Each day I would wake up wondering if that day was going to be the day my knee fell apart.

Instead, my knee got stronger. Although I didn't have a completely functioning patellar tendon, the hamstring tendon that was used to help reinforce the original surgery provided enough scaffolding for scar tissue to begin forming in place of the patellar. The type of training I was now undergoing forced my body to adapt to the stress by forming scar tissue with a sense of urgency. The more I pushed myself in training, my body would then respond by creating more "functional scar tissue."

It's quite ironic, considering I spent four months in Arizona to break down scar tissue that was impeding the function of my knee. Now, new scar tissue was being formed that allowed me to re-establish a high level of function. The human body is designed to heal, but we have to first give it what it needs to do so. The physical challenges I was putting my body through, along with the shift in my mental health, were the best medication for me.

But I had reached a saturation point with my time in Columbus. I was physically stronger and mentally in a great place, but I couldn't run. Yea, I looked like Michael Johnson running the 100 meters when I was on the underwater treadmill, but when I had to actually run over the ground, it looked like I had one leg that was six inches shorter than the other.

Had I wanted to switch careers and move in to powerlifting, I had a future. But I was a football player and the ability to run is a baseline requirement in the job description. I thought my inability to run was due to a lack of strength, but that hypothesis was slowly dispelled over time as my strength levels were inching closer to personal all-time bests.

The issue wasn't related to strength. My problems were both anatomical and neurological. The infection had decimated the tissue and cartilage in my knee, along with destroying the myelin sheath that protected the nerves. The anatomy of my knee had completely changed.

A key function of the patellar tendon is to hold down the kneecap. Considering I had no true patellar tendon, my kneecap was able to float up and position itself just above the end of my femur. Imagine taking your kneecap and moving it up two inches from where it currently resides. This is where my kneecap sits permanently.

This small anatomical shift creates significant issues. My kneecap resting so high shortened the length of my quadriceps and greatly affected my power output when extending my lower leg. It had become extremely difficult to build muscle mass in my lower quadriceps.

The resulting dysfunction was my knee collapsing whenever it would bend to the point where the knee would begin to fall over the toe. So imagine going down stairs with your right leg leading, the knee on your left leg will end up in a position where the knee is beyond the toe as you progressively descend down the stairs. This is when my leg would shut down. I wasn't able to function in this position. This was the first issue that was leading to my inability to run.

The second issue was a neurological one. There's a fatty coating around our nerves that's called the myelin sheath. It's what protects our nerves and allows for signaling from our brain to reach all parts of the body. If you take a close look at the cable on your cellular phone charger, there's a plastic coating that wraps around the wires that comprise the actual cable. When the charger is plugged in to a power source, the power source is then able to send a current through the wires and in to your phone battery.

Our nervous system operates in the same fashion with the brain acting as the power source and our nerves as the cables. Now, envision yourself taking a paring knife in one hand and your phone charger's cable in the other hand. You then begin to shave away bits of the plastic coating wrapped around the cable, now leaving the wires inside completely exposed. Congratulations, you have ruined your phone charger.

This is what the infection had achieved with my nerves. The result was a less clean signal being sent to muscles and proprioceptors inside the muscles. I wasn't able to contract the muscles in my lower quadriceps as effectively, or track where my knee was in space. I could manage these conditions at a slow rate of speed, such as when lifting weights. But I couldn't manage them when at a high rate of speed, such as when running.

These two issues were going to require a more refined

approach and time to overcome. The bright side: I wasn't close to giving up and I had all the time in the world.

I believe Arizona has one of the most forward-thinking wellness and medical communities in the world. So I left Columbus and headed back to Arizona; because I knew much of what I was going to need moving forward would be found there, and if not, the networks of others would lead me in the right direction. I had no idea how amazing the healing and learning journey I was about to embark on would become.

18 CHAPTER

BUILDING MY NETWORK

It didn't take long for my house to begin looking like a laboratory. There were cold lasers, infrared heat lamps, magnetic sleeping blankets, cold compression machines, sound therapy units, muscle stimulators, salt lamps and any other "cutting edge" piece of machinery that was available.

It didn't even need to be "cutting edge." If it was billed as a tool to help "heal" the body, I bought it. There was even a candle I would burn that was supposed to create a "healing environment." Sounded good to me; I bought the store's whole supply. I'd guesstimate I invested more than $300,000 in equipment I thought would help make me better.

Did they all deliver as promised? No, they didn't. But I do believe they all had a cumulative effect on my healing and mental psyche. Maybe the candles were bullshit, but my house did smell great, so there's that.

Regardless, I was learning how to take care of myself. My trust in others at this point was nonexistent. I would wake up, ride my bike, do my strengthening exercises, stretch, then begin treating myself with my arsenal of equipment. Between eating, taking supplements, riding my bike, and treatments, my entire days were full. My day would begin at 5:00 a.m. and end at 9:00 p.m. This had become my full-time job. It was a maniacal schedule and pace I was on, but it was what I needed.

I spent a couple weeks taking care of myself, but I knew there'd come a time when I had to get back under expert guidance. Because I ordered so many pieces of therapy equipment, I would meet all sorts of really knowledgeable and connected salespeople.

One of the saleswomen I met was a naturopath by the name of Dr. Sonja Peterson. She was a Canadian and it seemed every Canadian in the Phoenix area knew each other. Dr. Peterson would become a valuable resource in my recovery, as well as introduce me to another Canadian, Ian Danney.

Ian is one of the brightest individuals I have ever known. There are people you read about who are brilliant in so many different areas that it becomes impossible to place a single label on them; he is one of those rare people. Ian was so much more than a "strength coach." As a former Olympic bobsled athlete with a degree in organic chemistry, Ian understood the psyche of an elite level athlete, and viewed development through a broad scientific set of lenses. Ian is world-class in the weight room, physical therapy, biomechanics, nutrition and supplementation.

Some of you may be thinking, "Well if he's that good, why haven't I ever heard of him?" I was once this misinformed. I quickly realized that some of the best sports performance experts in the world are unknown to the masses. There's a complete underground network of specialists who aren't interested in writing books, acquiring social media followers, or being seen on television. I know, the term "underground" can invoke assumptions of less-than-aboveboard activity, but that's not the case in this instance. Many of these high level experts possess a similar disposition as artists and musicians where in their minds the "work" is all that matters. Ian was a master artist, and I was the perfect canvas for him.

The time I would spend with Ian was extensive and expensive. We began working with each other in July of 2007 and continued throughout 2008. My investment between Ian, naturopaths, traveling, and treatments added another $600,000 to my running tally. Yes, I had insurance through the team, but all of my training and therapy methods at the time were not covered by insurance. If I wanted to see this mission through, it was going to cost me, and I was perfectly fine with that. Often times, the best investment you can make is in yourself.

The first milestone I was working toward was getting myself ready to pass an NFL physical. I knew the only way I would ever be cleared to play was if Dr. Warren cleared me to do so.

He had already made it very clear to me where he stood on my future odds of playing. If I was going to change his mind, I couldn't be in good shape; I needed to be in phenomenal shape.

It was a hope of mine to make enough strides the first couple of months to get Dr. Warren to pass me on a physical and play at some point in the 2007 season. Those prospects were quickly dashed when I realized how far I had to go. Regaining my function was going to be a test of time, not will.

The problem in dealing with nerve damage is it requires time to heal — assuming it ever does. With the nerves not signaling properly, it was difficult to build muscle and increase my running and movement skills.

Another issue was pain management. The harder I pushed my damaged joint, the more pain and inflammation would become an issue. I could train really hard on one day, but would sometimes need up to a week to recover. These circumstances created a highly uncertain timetable. Scheduling a return for Week 4 for of the 2007 season turned into rescheduling for Week 8, and then to Week 12. Finally the season was over. I'd go on to miss the entire 2007 season. Now being two years out of football, the prospects of a return were getting slim, but I never lost focus on my goal.

19 CHAPTER

CLEARED TO RESUME FOOTBALL

The 2007 NFL season may have been a wash for me in terms of getting back on the field, but it was far from a wash in terms of my learning and healing. Was I recovering at the rate I may have wanted to? No. But considering I was attempting to glue back a leg that I had nearly lost, I wasn't working for a recovery. I was working for a miracle.

The entire 2007 season was spent training six days a week, getting treatments from a wide variety of soft tissue experts, receiving intravenous vitamin therapies, and traveling the world to see other elite performance experts who were specialists in an assortment of disciplines.

Between Arizona, Canada, and Germany, my time — and frequent flyer miles — was full. I slowly found myself beginning to not miss football and enjoying this journey I was on. Yes, I wanted to play, but I knew that my desire to play was not going to get me through each day. It was going to be my adherence to the process that would give me my best opportunity, and that's all I wanted — an opportunity.

You may have heard many former players note the locker room environment is what they miss the most from their playing days. Well, I was never a "locker room" kind of guy. My mindset didn't allow me to partake in much of the banter and camaraderie. I just wasn't social.

What I missed was the rush of competing. There's nothing like the thrill of preparing to whip another man's ass. As a player I loved the weight room, studying film, practice (sometimes), and the mental preparation required to play at a high level. That's what I missed about my career, but I had this void filled with the challenges I was facing. My body had become the most formidable opponent I had ever faced. If I were going to conquer my latest adversary, it would require the same adherence to tactics that enabled me to dominate my on-field opponents. Game day was no longer just on Sunday; every day was my game time.

If my return to football was going to happen, it had to be the 2008 season. My first significant milestone was the first offseason minicamp. I'd have to first get Dr. Warren's blessing, then waltz in to the Browns facility as if nothing ever happened. The latter was going to be more of an improbable challenge. My 10 months of training had me very confident this was all going to become a reality.

Was I running like Usain Bolt? No, but I was moving like a football player. In all of my football specific drills I was very close to being my old self. The time had come to put all of the chips on the table.

I booked my flight to New York City for an appointment with Dr. Warren. He had no clue what I had been doing or what I was now capable of. The last time he saw me was 11 months prior, when I was hoping he'd agree to perform surgery on my knee. Needless to say, I was excited to have him see how far I had come.

When the nurse came to take me back to the waiting room, I was as anxious and nervous as I'd been on a game day.

"Wow, you look great," she said.

She was right. I had been living in a weight room, eating custom meals for a year; I was basically in a "performance incubator." I was 305 pounds and teetering between 9 and 10 percent body fat.

"How have things been going?" she asked.

My reply was less than poetic, "Well, it's been good. Just living life."

Yea, if you were to qualify "life" as a maniacal effort to do the impossible, then I was an upstanding citizen in the small city called Bat Shit Crazy.

It wasn't long before Dr. Warren came bursting through the door.

"LeCharles, it's great to see you," he said in his very usual dry tone.

This was my moment. I had to show him what I could do. I sprang up from the chair, walked over to the bed, and jumped on top of it. I then jumped down from the table and started doing air squats to show him how functional I had become. He stared at me as if I were crazy. Well, he was partly right; I was crazy with a purpose. Once I completed my circus routine, he had me sit on the examination table to begin an actual medical exam. I couldn't contain myself. All the while, I was babbling on about all of the things I was doing in training and how far I had come. I was nearly out of breath by the time he completed poking and prodding my knee in amazement.

He took a step back and said, "What have you been doing?"

It was apparent he hadn't heard a single word I had said, which was probably a good thing. I calmly gathered myself and began to reiterate all that I had said, but this time like an actual adult and not a two-year-old attempting to explain the theory of relativity.

I could tell by the bewildered look on his face that he was impressed not just with my progress, but also with my conviction to this process. Remember, this was the man that told me to "go buy a boat" because he believed my career was over. Now I was about to attempt to get an elite medical expert to reverse their diagnosis.

"Doc, I want to play football. I know I can do it. But I need you to clear me," I said.

He took another step backward and folded his arms. All the while his gaze was locked on to my knee. He slowly began to shake his head left to right. I knew this wasn't a "no," but his astonishment at my progress subconsciously coming through.

"You really want to do this?" he asked.

At this point, I knew I had him.

"Doc, I told you I am not buying a damn boat. Please let me

try," I said.

There was a tense silence in the room. He then said the magical words, "Ok, I will clear you."

I jumped up and gave him the biggest hug. It was extremely hard for me to not run up and down the hallways screaming at the top of my lungs. I thanked him profusely and promised to keep working hard.

I walked out of his office with a handwritten note that read: "LeCharles is cleared to resume all football related activities."

I had done it!

20 CHAPTER

SAY HELLO TO THE BAD GUY

Spring 2008, and the Browns were set to kick off their first minicamp of the season. I was all set to show up at minicamp to proudly present my clearance note to the team.

My emotions were mixed at this point. There were clearly some unaddressed issues that needed to be cleared up, but my focus was on getting back to playing, not dealing with drama. I knew there was a team meeting at 8:00 A.M., so I decided that was when I'd re-appear as a member of the Cleveland Browns football club.

My heart was racing when I pulled into the parking lot of the facility. It had been almost two years since I was in a football team environment. At this point in my life, it was the longest I had ever been away from football.

There were new players and coaches in the building since I was last there. I had no clue as to what the reception would be, but at the same time, I didn't care. I had never been one to care much about what others thought of me, but this personality trait had become more pronounced than ever due to all that I had gone through.

For the most part, I was alone on this journey. None of the medical staff, coaches, or players called to check on how I was coping. The business and the game had moved on without me.

It's the reality of show business. I knew a lot of people were going to be uncomfortable with me around and I partly relished that fact. But I couldn't overcome the anxious "first day of school" feeling I had as I sat in the parking lot. I watched from the parking lot as players trickled in to the building. Some of the faces were more familiar than others. My plan was to walk in at the last minute. This was in hope of avoiding much of the awkward small talk players like to engage in. I was in no mood to be adorned with fake handshakes and hugs.

It was 7:57 when I began to make my way toward the door. I could feel my heart racing more and more with each step I took. As I stepped into the building the different energies that work their way around football facilities were omnipresent. I had forgotten how tense and uptight the business of football truly was. The energies of uncertainty, youthful excitement, nervousness, anxiety, unease, and fear is a distinct combination of energies that players adapt to, but never truly understand until they are away from the game.

It's like living in a house with a sewage problem. The house stinks, but you have adjusted to the smell, so you don't realize how bad it truly smells. This is until you leave the house for a period of time and come back in. Suddenly, the funk hits you.

Players learn how to thrive in emotional chaos that in "normal" circumstances is considered an unhealthy work environment.

At 7:59 I walked in the meeting room as Romeo Crennel was just getting ready to address the team.

The moment was gloriously awkward. It was as if a ghost had walked in the room. I scanned the room for a seat, and there was one in the front row next to linebacker Andra Davis. I was so relieved to find an immediate seat next to one of the few people in this business I truly respected as a person and player. Andra was one of the good guys. He and I briefly exchanged pleasantries as Romeo took the microphone to begin the meeting.

The meeting felt really brief. I don't recall much of what was discussed because throughout the entire meeting I was thinking to myself, "I can't believe I'm here." Was it awkward, yes, but it felt so good to in my mind be back on track to achieve what I thought was so important to my life's happiness.

I was ready to get back to work, but quickly realized this wasn't going to be as simple as handing the team my permission slip and all being good. It was brought to my attention that I would need to pass the team-conditioning test to be allowed to practice.

I thought this was extremely strange considering this was minicamp and not training camp. The point of minicamp is to get back in to the groove of football in a relatively low intensity environment. Minicamp is where guys who are traditionally working themselves back from injury are able to gauge where they are without the pressure on the player and coaching staff of a looming season.

It was strange to be asked to pass a conditioning test at this point in the year. I was a bit concerned because my running mechanics were much better than they had been, but my "conditioning" hadn't been a focus for quite some time. Also, even when "healthy" I wasn't known to be a fan of conditioning test.

Needless to say, I wasn't happy about this request but realized it was part of the game I knew I would have to play in order to get back to doing what I truly wanted to do, which was to play football.

The conditioning test was comprised of 20 40-yards sprints which all had to be completed in less than 5.5 seconds. It had turned into a complete spectacle.

The bulk of the executive staff was on hand along with the coaching staff, Jim Brown, the strength staff and team doctors. The entire thing was videotaped.

This clearly wasn't the typical conditioning test format. I was nervous enough about the testing itself, but the crowd made this feel like the main event. At that time I didn't understand why so many people were interested in watching a 300-pound man run a conditioning test. Looking back on it, it all made sense.

I had no clue at the time how many people were made to believe I would never play football again. It was as if they were in on a secret that I was not. Suddenly, there I was back inside of the facility looking better than ever. This was clearly a mystery to many and was something they had to see with their own eyes.

I made 18 of the twenty on time, but missed the last two. I failed the test, but I was far from upset about it. I had done much better than I had anticipated and it was my understanding that other players who were completely healthy had failed their test as well.

The difference between me and the others was those players were allowed to practice. I was not. This was when I knew the battle I was fighting was much bigger than my ability to pass a physical or conditioning test and then play football. If it were solely up to the coaches, I would have been allowed to practice. But a rarely understood component of the operations of a NFL franchise is the fact that many of the decisions made are not made by coaches. Yes, the coaches take all of the day-to-day heat, but often they are merely taking orders from non-football experts.

I was told I wouldn't be able to practice, so I packed my bags and headed back to Arizona to train. I was fed some political bullshit about them being "concerned for my long term health" and "you really need to pass the conditioning test." Fine, if they wanted me to pass that ridiculous test, that's what I would do. In my mind, I knew that wouldn't be enough, but at least I was now back at the table to even discuss the possibility of playing again.

I know some of you may not completely understand why a team wouldn't want a good player around, but this wasn't exactly a normal circumstance. I wasn't just "any player." The combination of my accomplishments on the field, contract value, being from Cleveland, and the medical mishappenings made my situation unique because it left a lot of people in a vulnerable position.

It was a perfect storm of chaos. There were jobs, ego, reputations, and a lot of money at risk. This is why it was best for me to just "go away."

But I wasn't ready to do that.

Once back in Arizona, my focus was on continuing to get bigger, faster, stronger, and to pass that damn conditioning test. There wasn't much changed in my training routine. But there was an increased sense of urgency for two reasons. I had gotten a taste of the football environment again and there was another minicamp coming up in about five weeks. These two combined factors pushed me in to overdrive.

I was closer than ever to seeing this journey completely through. I could feel it. But there was something else I was beginning to feel.

A small part of me began to wonder if this was all worth it. The emotional drain was beginning to take a toll. I had weathered these instances of intense highs and lows, as if to develop what I thought was cynicism toward the process. It was as if I was always anticipating the worst-case scenario.

But this wasn't a factor at this point. What I didn't fully understand at the time was that I was developing a higher level of thinking. I was learning how to fully study the landscape of every situation I was placed in. Instead of operating on blind faith and relying solely on intensity as the primary method of execution, I was learning how to think outside of myself.

This is a high level thinking skill that American developmental psychologist John Flavell termed metacognition. In a nutshell, metacognition is your ability to think about how you think. It's your ability to strategize, organize, and implement plans of action to achieve a desired outcome. A part of metacognition understands when and where to use particular strategies. But you must first be able to see realities from a multitude of angles and vantage points that typically extend beyond yourself.

Every day of our lives we are placed in situations where our metacognitive skills can be developed, but we often miss these opportunities because our emotions or implicit biases towards certain situations drive our thought processes. My emotionally driven self had me choosing death over life at one point in this journey. This was because I couldn't see the forest for the trees.

The many twists and turns along the way allowed me to develop a higher level of emotional reactionary skills, coping mechanisms, strategies, and new methods of execution that didn't require me to work "harder," but allowed me to work "smarter." This is a skill that so many of us from all walks of life fail to develop.

The time back in Arizona seemed to be so short. Five weeks were up and it was time for me to head back to Cleveland. There was no doubt I was going to pass the conditioning test this time; I had run it twice a week for the past five weeks.

The only thing I wondered was what excuse could they possibly come up with this time to keep me from practicing. I knew the coaching staff didn't care about a conditioning test; they only cared if I could play football. So I came up with the idea that would placate the executives upstairs and the coaching staff. I would run the conditioning test, and then complete a full padded workout against players. The latter was something I knew the coaches would want to see and would satisfy in their minds my readiness to play football. I knew my best opportunity to get back on the field was if I passed my conditioning test and threw in the added bonus of having the football coaches see me back playing football.

I flew back to Cleveland a few days prior to the start of minicamp to give myself extra time to adjust to the three-hour time difference between Arizona and Ohio. I wanted to be sure I had removed any plausible scenario for me to not be at my best.

The test was scheduled to take place after hours. It was my assumption they didn't want any players in the building when I was there. The environment was much more subdued this time. There was no crowd, but Ian made the trip with me to Cleveland and was on hand at the test. I wanted him to take me through the warm-up protocol he had designed specifically for me. Once again, I did this because I didn't want any "what if" scenario to haunt me if God forbid something had happened to prevent me from passing this test.

To my surprise, there was a former teammate from my time in New Orleans, who was around the facility and wanted to run the test with me as show of support. Shaun Smith was a very large defensive tackle I had grown close to when we played for the Saints. He had become a free agent and signed with the Browns over the time I was rehabbing. Having him run the test with me gave me a great pace partner. It also reminded me that, yes, the NFL is a business, but it's still driven by people and relationships.

Bad teams are often the net result of poor relationships within the architecture of team design. Having the support of Shaun gave me a tremendous boost in confidence. He was someone who knew me as a person and player. Shaun understood how important this was to me. He and I crushed the conditioning test, together.

With the first part of my plan completed, I knew the second part would be the most important. As the old saying goes, good news tends to travel slowly. The fact I passed the conditioning test wasn't going to be news that would make its way around the building at the same speed had I failed it.

This gave me some time to seek out the head coach and propose my idea. I wandered around the building in search of Romeo Crennel for what seemed like hours. This was probably due to the fact my legs were tired and I was actually a bit nervous about my proposition. I knew if he allowed me to do this, and I did well, this would place the coaches in a difficult spot, because it would be much harder for management to continue selling their narrative that I would "never play football again."

I didn't care. Whatever was going to happen, it had to be on record that I gave everything I had to make their narrative untrue.

I eventually found Romeo in his office. I can't really explain why didn't I look there in the first place. I had looked everywhere he wouldn't be before finding him in the place he was most likely to be. I know, it's silly, but in hindsight this was just my way of stalling.

I walked in and said, "Coach, I have an idea. Why don't you bring out a few defensive linemen and let do some live drills with full pads on?"

He looked stunned by what had just come out of my mouth. This was a man who had been led to believe that my playing days were over. We hadn't had any contact. He could only surmise my future based on information he heard from others, even though those "others" hadn't spoken with me to know what was true and not true.

"You know, that's a good idea. Let's do that," he said.

At that very moment my heart sank to my feet. I didn't plan on it being that easy. There was a script in my mind I was prepared to follow that consisted of at least five different rebuttals to excuses I was planning to hear. Remember, I had grown accustomed to things having to be done the hard way. This had gone way better than I had anticipated.

"In fact, let's do it tomorrow morning," he said.

It was go time.

"Perfect, see you in the morning," I replied.

So many emotions came over me as I walked down the hall and down the back staircase of the facility. I hadn't put on football pads in two years, and there I was less than 24 hours away from engaging in live drills. This was what I wanted. This was what all of the work had prepared me for. There was no doubt in my mind I was going to do well, but I couldn't help but wonder if my body would hold up. Yes, I was in great physical shape, but it felt as if I was taking a prototype racecar and entering it in the Indy 500, without any test laps.

There was no other option. If I was going to fail, it wasn't going to be from a lack of trying.

I could hardly sleep that night. I spent much of the night watching old game film of myself. I had to remember who I was.

For years I was not a football player. I was a guy hoping to play football again. Those are two completely different mindsets. As a football player there was rarely an occasion where my mind wasn't inundated with visions of me dominating opponents or playing back instances in games where I wish I could go back and undo past mistakes. My headspace was a constant video reel of football.

As a guy aspiring to resume my career, my focus was on the day to day. I lived one surgery to the next, one rep to the next, one set to the next, one meal to the next, and then one emotion to the next. The process consumed me.

Now, it was time to turn the football player switch back on.

21 CHAPTER

I KNEW IT WAS TIME TO MOVE ON

We were scheduled to begin the workout at 9 a.m., so I arrived at the facility at 5:30.

This was my personal game day. I wanted to follow the identical format I had used in my past game day routines. When I played for the Saints, my breakfast was oatmeal with fruit, and I would arrive at the stadium four hours before kickoff.

At away games I'd catch a cab to the opposing team's stadium. I had to be in the stadium first. Typically, I would be fully dressed two hours before the ball was teed up. This allowed me to "relax;" I would sit in my locker and visualize playing the perfect game. Did I ever play the "perfect" game? I didn't. But this routine surely placed me in a better position to do so.

The emotion of putting on my full uniform was a bit overwhelming. I didn't anticipate this. It had been more than two years since I had on a full uniform. There was so much uncertainty. I had accomplished what so many thought would never be done again.

I also wasn't just putting on a uniform. I was putting on a

freaking Cleveland Browns uniform. This was my dream. Although this wasn't an official game day uniform, it did not matter to me.

These two elements pushed my emotions to a nuclear tipping point. I didn't know who coach Crennel was going to bring out to line up across from me; whoever it was, they had no I idea what they were getting themselves into.

As I walked on the turf at the team's indoor field, I was not nervous for the first time in my entire football career. This was strange. There had never been a time when I wasn't nervous stepping on a field. It didn't matter if it was practice or Monday Night Football. I was in constant fear of being embarrassed by another man. The fear is what pushed me to be better. It didn't paralyze me. It molded me. But it wasn't there anymore. At the time, I didn't know what it was, because it was so unfamiliar. I just knew that it was 'go time,' and anyone who lined up across from me was going to get eaten.

The workout lasted about 30 minutes. It was 30 minutes of coach Crennel signaling with his hands what he wanted me to do. If he pointed to his right shoulder, this was the signal to "reach block" the defensive player. When he pointed to the middle of his chest, this was my cue to "base block" the defensive player. The final signal was a point to his left shoulder; this is where I had to make contact with the defensive player, and then run to the linebacker and strike him. The time also included a one-on-one pass rush session, where the defensive player would rush at me as if he were trying to sack the quarterback. This entire session was done in full pads and at full speed.

I kicked the shit out of those guys.

When it ended Romeo Crennel walked over to me and said, "That was quite impressive. I will see you at practice in the morning."

Well, there aren't enough words in any language to describe how I felt. Passing the conditioning test paled in comparison; what I had just finished was football. A conditioning test didn't prove I could play football. To hear those words from a man like Romeo Crennel, who had been coaching football longer than I had been alive, was the approval I had been longing for. It was the "nod" that made this entire journey worthwhile.

The next day was the first day of minicamp. It was a complete media circus. I recall staying in the weight room adjacent to the indoor facility for as long as I could. There was zero part of me that felt like playing "nice" to a few of the media members. I hadn't forgotten their articles and comments that fanned the flames of many Browns fans who perceived me in a less than noble light. But a part of me didn't blame them. Individuals inside the organization were feeding them mistruths to create a false narrative. Either way, it was going to be a challenge to keep a professional decorum, thus I wanted to limit the amount of time they would have to ask me questions.

Eventually I made my way to the field. Cameras, recorders, and note pads immediately circled me as media members fired away with their questions. The media who had seemed to know so much about what I was dealing with and who had the strongest opinions about me as a person, they were quiet as church mice.

The energy from the general group reporters oozed awe. They had all heard so much, but didn't know what to believe. Frankly, there are some awful people in the Cleveland media, but overall, there are more really good people. Nobody in the media wanted to see me hurt. There wasn't a single person in the media who didn't want to see me be successful in Cleveland. But they are still human beings. Many of them have lived firsthand through much of the organization's heartbreak, and it's hard for them to overcome their "woe is me" mentality. My situation was just another example of the "curse" many Cleveland fans and media members subscribed to. I don't blame them for their actions. I understand it, now.

I marched across the field to begin my first day of practice. It was all a bit surreal. As I stood in the back to watch some of the other offensive linemen go through their footwork drills, I couldn't help but flash back through the myriad emotions I had experienced through the years. The highs and lows all brought me back to this moment I had been longing for.

But it wasn't what I thought it would be. I was anticipating an overwhelming resurgence of excitement for the game that would continue to carry me through my career. Instead, there was a profound moment of clarity that had me questioning if all of this was worth it.

My turn came around to go through some of the footwork drills. I lined up and did exactly what the drill called for. It didn't feel right. My legs were a little sore from the workout from the day before, but the "feel" I am referring to is an emotional feel. My mind wouldn't allow me to enjoy the moment. I had a keen understanding of what I was getting myself back into. Football wasn't a hobby to me. It was all encompassing. There were key aspects of my life and family that I was more than willing to sacrifice to place myself in the best situation to be successful. This wasn't exactly healthy; it simply worked for me. But the key difference between the person I was before the injury and the person I had become in the aftermath was developing perspective.

All of the people I had forsaken to achieve my goals as a player — they were all of the people who were there for me when it looked as if my football career was over and football had moved on without me. I wasn't ready or willing to go back to living my life with a singular focus. As I stood on the back of the goal line surveying all that was going on in front of me, I thought to myself, "I almost died for this shit and none of these muthafuckas gave a shit."

At that very moment I knew I was done.

After all I had been through, this may have seemed like a difficult moment. No, this was a very easy realization. Nobody cared. I wasn't willing to lose my kids and family for that shit. I wasn't going to allow myself back into that trap.

The next morning I woke up, put on a collared shirt with khaki pants, and grabbed a carry-on size roller suitcase. My plan was to go in, clean out my locker, and tell the general manager to release me. My mind was solely on executing my plan.

My mother dropped me off at the facility at about 5 A.M. If I had driven myself I would have had an opportunity to change my mind. This was a military strategy accredited to Hernando Cortes and Alexander the Great. Both leaders were faced with seemingly insurmountable odds as the opposition outnumbered their armies. The orders to "burn the boats" ensured their troops' options were limited to death or victory. By not having an escape option, I had to follow through.

I was surprisingly calm as I cleaned out my locker before heading upstairs to the office of general manager Phil Savage. The locker was loaded with supplements that were outdated, a playbook that looked like a telephone book, and enough shoes to outfit an entire high school offensive line. No one else was in the locker room, so I didn't have to deal with an onslaught of inquiries about what I was doing. Once I stuffed my suitcase, I began to slowly make my way to the general manager's office. I had seen other players make this trip on cut day under non-voluntary circumstances. Here I was making the identical trip to the guillotine, but as a volunteer.

My rolling suitcase made a loud clunking sound as I pulled it up the back stairway. The stage seemed to be set. On any given typical day there would be players, trainers, or at least a coach you'd make contact with within a short time of being inside the facility. I had been in the building for at least 20 minutes and had not run into anyone.

The first person I made contact with was the general manager's secretary.

"Hello, is Phil around?" I said. She looked up and smiled.

"Good morning! Let me see if he's available for you," she replied.

She dipped into his office and immediately returned.

"Go right on in, sweetie," she said.

I took a deep breath and walked in.

"Phil, I think it's best for you to release me."

He looked stunned. Regardless of the circumstances, it's not every day a player asks to be fired. This was something he clearly wasn't anticipating.

I didn't let him respond right away.

"There's a lot of damage that's been done to this relationship that's not going to be fixed," I said. "It's best for us to go our separate ways."

If it sounds like the same commentary you've heard or used in a breakup with a significant other, you're correct. Because that's what it felt like. This was a relationship that went horribly wrong. We both knew it was best for it to end, which is why Phil conceded without much objection. Our conversation concluded with a bit of small talk and a handshake, and just like that, I was no longer a Cleveland Brown.

It wasn't long before my phone was ringing with opportunities to continue my career elsewhere. The first coach I spoke with later that day was Mike Tomlin of the Pittsburgh Steelers. This was an intriguing conversation due to my understanding the legacy of great centers in Pittsburgh and the fact I would play against the Browns twice a year. A part of me relished the chance to have a little "get back" of my own.

The other part of me didn't want to betray my hometown, Cleveland. Yes, I had personal animosity against some of the fan base and the Browns organization, but Cleveland was my home. Many of the "fans" who took issue with me weren't even Clevelanders. The organization was filled with transient workers who were only loyal to the person signing their checks.

Cleveland was my home. I had no immediate plans to leave. All of my family is still in Cleveland. Some of the best relationships I have are with people still in Cleveland. That city will always be a part of me. The opportunity to play in Pittsburgh just didn't feel right.

In the end, I realized my connection to football had been altered. No longer was I a "football player." My passion for playing had faded, but a new passion was born.

I fell in love with the game behind the game. Some will call it the "business of football," but it's so much more than that. Yes, I learned a tremendous amount about the business side of the NFL through my experiences, especially after filing a lawsuit against the Browns. I saw firsthand how expendable players are, but also how the machinery of the NFL can mobilize to work for and against players.

So many players are ignorant to all of the unseen factors that play significant roles in their careers. As athletes, we see the game as a meritocracy where the hardest workers are the ones afforded opportunity. This is the furthest thing from the truth.

I had experienced the highest level of individual rejoicings in this business, while also experiencing the lowest levels of tragedy. My time in the NFL was a complete oxymoron. But it was preparing me for my life's true calling.

During the years of working to build back my body, I established a deep appreciation for human performance. My views on how the body worked changed once mine no longer could do the things it used to be able to.

"You don't know what you got until it's gone" is the adage.

That was the absolute truth for me.

22 CHAPTER

TIME TO GIVE BACK TO THE GAME

Like many former athletes, I didn't know what I wanted to do now that I was a "former football player." Luckily I wasn't in a situation where I had to take on opportunities that weren't truly the best for me.

This is a trap so many former athletes fall victim to. The notion of being "set for life" is not reality. It doesn't matter how much money an athlete earns in his or her career, everyone leaves their respective game at a young age. There's a lot of life left to live.

The same passion and drive that created an opportunity to excel in professional athletics has to be funneled into something constructive. The dream of golfing and sitting by the pool is a façade. Usually, athletes who believe their professional career is the key to creating this illusory post-career lifestyle are the ones who don't make it.

The highest-level achievers are those who don't play the game for money, but use the platform as a chance to pursue a deep-seated element of who they are as people. The result of this pursuit is where the money comes into the equation. These inherent traits don't magically go away when the sun sets on your time as a professional athlete.

For those who don't have a constructive outlet, a destructive option often fills the void. This is where we see many former athletes across all sports in precarious financial, social or marital circumstances.

I knew my inner drive wasn't going to land me anywhere positive if I did not center my focus. My plan was complex, but simple.

I wanted to give back to the game that had given me so much. I needed to share with players the knowledge I accrued. But it had to be on my own terms. I refused to operate under anyone's rules, only the ones I created. That meant coaching was not an option.

The idea of becoming a sports agent flashed across my mind, but I don't exactly care for the industry. I can't speak for the sports agent business models outside of football, but in the NFL where contracts aren't worth the paper they're written on, player representation is a pseudo-value based industry that rarely creates value for athletes. Far too many athletes fall for the shenanigans.

These big and strong men work their entire lives to reach the NFL, then give away their sovereignty to an industry that had zero impact on getting them there — and will have zero impact in keeping them there.

A football player's value is based on the work he invests in himself, and, in many cases, luck. If a player is fortunate enough to become a free agent, the market will always dictate what a player is worth.

I was the best interior offensive lineman on the market when I hit free agency. There was a need for my services and there wasn't anyone available at the time who came close to doing the things I could do. My services went for a premium. Had there been three or four other good players available not quite at my performance level, my market value would have been hurt. Teams would have been perfectly fine paying less for a good offensive lineman instead of paying a premium for a great one.

A football agent doesn't create value; talent supply and demand does. I didn't feel comfortable being a part of an industry that pushes a false narrative to athletes. My vision wasn't to become a part of the problem, but part of the solution and seeing athletes maximize their careers and lives.

My vision: to change the landscape of how offensive line players were developed at all levels, to shift how offensive line coaches taught the skill, to change how the careers of professional offensive linemen were managed, and to help as many people along the way that I humanly could.

I wanted to have an impact on the game and to change lives. This is where my life was headed.

My first step was to open a training center to develop offensive line athletes. This facility would be the first of its kind in the world.

My new business started slowly, the way most "new"

concepts start. The slow growth gave me the opportunity to build the skills required to complete my vision. Like any new entrepreneur, I wanted the business to blow up overnight.

That didn't happen, thankfully.

My venture began with a four seven-year-olds who paid $20 dollars each for 90 minutes of "training" on Saturday mornings. The place was empty the rest of the week. I drove to 25 high schools throughout Northeast Ohio to meet with coaches with the hopes of them sending more young athletes.

There's a Bible verse I relied on: Job 8:7. "And though your start was small, your end will be very great."

This was my reminder to stay focused on the big picture and not let myself get washed out by early struggles. Was it easy? No. But the fight was better than the alternative, which was failure.

A critical component in fulfilling my vision was for me to begin building skill sets and refining personality traits needed for success. As an athlete, I wasn't exactly what you would consider "social." There wasn't a lot for me to say, so I didn't say much. The acquaintances I developed in the locker rooms weren't of much substance.

I was going to need to learn how to communicate more effectively with people I didn't know. The ability to build meaningful relationships was vital for the vision I held.

Where is the best place for a former athlete to learn to communicate? The media. It was the easiest place to find employment that matched the background experience I had at the time.

I began working in radio, television, and writing for several major outlets, among them ESPN, Big Ten Network, AOL Fanhouse, and NFL Network. The lessons learned in communication, networking and understanding the media from the inside was invaluable. The same way I studied opponents as a player, I studied and rubbed elbows with respected media members.

My classroom was sports talk radio, social media, television networks, and sporting events. I worked my way into hosting a popular radio show in Cleveland. This allowed me to connect with fans in a way I had never experienced. I began to understand the psychology of what it meant to be a "fan."

Here is where I learned how voice inflection, timing, and rhythm played a role in how a message was received. The delivery is everything. I earned a figurative master's degree in communication as a member of the media. All of the skills I acquired would set the stage for how I developed my teaching, communication, and relationship-building skills with my athletes.

Many former athletes wrongly assume they know all they need to know about their sport. I didn't want to make that mistake. I acquired two types of knowledge during my years as an athlete.

First, I knew what I learned from coaches. This is called explicit knowledge. A coach would tell me to do something, so I did it. It may have worked for me not because of the quality of information, but because I was more talented than my peers. Explicit knowledge is dangerous for former players to utilize as the sole base for establishing their coaching careers because it sets the stage for less talented players to not be successful under their coaching methods.

The second knowledge base came from my earned on-field experience, which was tremendously valuable but wasn't something I could give to another person. This is called tacit knowledge. Tacit knowledge is why many former great athletes make the worst coaches. It's assumed they "know" the game. They do, but they don't know how to teach what they know. Michael Phelps can't give another swimmer his tacit knowledge earned during years of performing at an elite level. Phelps has a built-in unrivaled "feel" for the pool.

My goal was to marry my on-field explicit and tacit knowledge, while intertwining my newly formed tacit knowledge after losing the physical capabilities that made me the player I once was. All of those years of doctor visits, surgeries, rehabilitation, training and mental growth instilled in me a unique knowledge base that allowed me to see football through a totally different set of lenses.

One of the more important elements in seeing my vision through would be to substantiate this unique knowledge I acquired. My investments in seminars, clinics, books, film study and anything I felt was going add to my knowledge base on human performance was critical. Over time I became a certified strength and conditioning specialist, a sports nutritionist and a Fascial Stretch Therapist. I also earned certifications in Olympic weightlifting and Functional Movement Screening.

These credentials didn't magically turn me into an expert, but they did allow me to create distinctive mental scaffolding that connected my tacit and explicit knowledge bases in very unexpected ways. No longer was I a "former athlete."

I worked my way into a performance expert. The difference between the guy who just "used to play football" and a performance expert is analogous to the distinction between people with a driver's license versus a commercial driving license.

A person with a driver's license will possess basic knowledge about their vehicle, such as how to change a flat tire or when to get an oil change. They'll also have a solid understanding of routes to get them to and from their destinations.

Truck drivers require a deeper knowledge threshold. They need to know how to drive a 10-speed transmission. They need to read maps, to understand mechanical aspects of the truck, know federal trucking regulations and how to dock a trailer. The list goes on.

I needed to be the "truck driver." I submerged myself in information about the mental, physical, emotional, nutritional, biomechanical and strength components required to build great athletes.

I knew I was a great football player, but I didn't know what made me different from many of my peers.

Today, I know the answer, and an important part of realizing my vision is to continue to become the person in other athletes' lives I wish the younger football-playing version of me had in his life.

23 CHAPTER

REBUILT TO DOMINATE

My vision has grown into an internationally recognized brand that has an impact on the lives and careers of athletes and coaches.

What I started with four 7-year-olds blossomed into LB Management LLC, a full-service management firm for more than 30 NFL offensive linemen.

My vision has extended to LB™ Design, which designs football equipment sold to NFL teams, major collegiate programs, high schools, and international football clubs.

Several colleges and NFL teams are utilizing OLP™ Consulting, which advances the development of coaches and players.

The quiet kid from Cleveland now runs Built to Dominate™ Seminars, which hosts domestic and international seminars to teach the principles and methods I've developed the past decade.

My digital platform — OLP™ Digital — allows me to leverage technology that reaches an audience and consumer base from around the world.

I'm able to continuously challenge myself through entrepreneurship in ways I never imagined, such as negotiating brand-extending deals with companies including Nike, Ford and Power Lift Equipment.

As a football player, I only wanted to be better than I was the week before. This mentality can create tunnel vision that's not conducive to holistic personal development, which is why I'm committed to extending academic opportunities to minority and financially impoverished inner-city males.

Through philanthropic endeavors, I've committed more than $3 million to academic endowments earmarked for non-athletes. Why specifically "non-athletes?" A good athlete never needs to look for someone to remind them of how "amazing" they are because of their ability to run fast or jump high. These same people are complicit in creating a self-limiting perspective for the athlete that ultimately ill-prepares them for life.

I want young men to know they can go beyond where their knees or jump shot can take them, and sometimes the most effective way to achieve this is to keep them away from the systematic programming that can take place in athletics.

I am not even close to fulfilling my life's purpose. Each morning I wake up with the same drive I had as an athlete. My biggest fear is to leave this earth with the feeling that my calling has not been completed. I've been given a very clear vision, and as of right now, my job is to have an impact on the lives of people within this like-minded community. Similar to my football career being the platform that propelled me to where I am today, this season of my life is another platform that is positioning me for what's next.

This may leave you with the question, "What's next for LeCharles?" A lot.

There were significant takeaways from my experience that have helped shape my life. I believe these lessons are beneficial to people far beyond the world of sports. I've consolidated these takeaways into 3 questions that help establish a foundation for personal development.

I ask myself these three questions prior to committing to any endeavor that could potentially have life-altering consequences. It may be a career change, opening a new business, or starting a family. Anything that could possibly shift your life from its current state to another needs to be filtered through a sieve that will help you determine what's best.

I believe many people don't reach their fullest potential not because of a lack of work ethic, but due to the inability to ask themselves the right questions prior to constraining themselves to a place in life that may be far beneath their potential. The flipside, many people fail because passion can be blinding. Passion often prevents us from asking the right questions because emotion, not reasoning, is in the driver's seat.

The ability to think critically is imperative to one's success or failure.

First, is it my sight or vision leading me?

If you're led by sight, you will never accomplish anything more than what you're led to believe you can, or what your circumstances will dictate possible. Unfortunately, many people are living their influences and not their lives. Some people have never been exposed to anything more than their environment, and often their lives become extensions of the missed opportunities, insecurities and deep-seated fears of the people around them. My father wasn't too keen on me going to college. It wasn't because he didn't want me to be successful; it was because he only completed second grade. He didn't see the value. Had I listened, I wouldn't be where I am today. The vision I had for my life required college. Your vision is usually going to be something that other people can't or aren't willing to see. This can't deter you. Remember, it's your vision, not theirs. When your heart and mind is set upon your vision, an unlimited world of possibilities opens up to you.

Second, do I have a "This-is-what-it's-going-to-take mindset?"

We all have an internal compass that helps us navigate life's twists and turns. Humans are wired for survival. The issue with most of us is that we've become overly domesticated. Instead of hunting for answers, we dine on the drive-thru satisfaction of excuses. When we have a clearly established vision, the hard part is identifying the level of sacrifice it will require, and then commit to those sacrifices. Let's say you want to lose 20 pounds to avoid becoming a Type 2 diabetic, and because you have always wanted to compete in a 5k run. You've been overweight your entire life, and you're a less than stellar athlete. Your friends and family chuckle when you go on your "diets," and you hate going to the gym because in your mind everyone is laughing at you. There needs to be a dramatic shift in your mindset to fulfill your vision.

Begin by asking yourself this: "What will it require for me to fulfill this goal?" If you do, there's a very good chance the answers will scare you. This fear will paralyze you and keep you from completing the task. Make a subtle shift in mindset. Don't ask what it will take; identify what it will take. You are now telling your brain this IS what I am going to do. It's no longer a question; it's a command. This slight shift moves us a bit closer to the primal versions of ourselves where instinct drives us toward solutions and not towards excuses. Imagine if I had asked myself: "What will it take to play football again?" That list of answers would be overwhelming. By telling myself "I am willing to do whatever it takes to play football again," I was able to meet every known and unknown challenge head on.

Third, and finally, am I willing to embrace the process?

Now that you have your vision outlined and you know what it's going to take, the final step is asking yourself if you're able to weather the storm. The ability to execute is the trait separating the haves from the have-nots. This is when you need to look yourself in the mirror and determine if the person looking back at you is ready for this fight.

The world that we live in thrives on creating false images. We see it every day on social media where people present the best versions of themselves or the version they wish existed. We've become desensitized to the need for honest and introspective self-dialogue. Society will lead you to believe everyone is capable of becoming the next Steve Jobs or mega-entrepreneur. This isn't true. The only thing we are able to become is the best version of who we are. But if you are never honest with yourself, how do you know what's the best version of who you are?

Things won't come easy. There will be major setbacks. It will be uncomfortable. People will laugh at you. You may lose sleep. It will hurt at times. Maybe you aren't comfortable taking risks, or you're not OK with some people not liking you. Even the strongest metal alloy has a melting point; you need to know yours.

The moment the doctor told me he wasn't sure I would keep my leg; my response was that I wanted to die. I melted. I learned from that experience to never allow any one thing to define who I am.

If you make the same mistake I did, you'll never discover your true self and will always be susceptible to losing everything, right at the time you are primed to gain it all.

Made in the USA
Lexington, KY
02 February 2019